MILITARY PILOT SHORTAGE

HEARING

BEFORE THE

SUBCOMMITTEE ON MILITARY PERSONNEL

OF THE

COMMITTEE ON ARMED SERVICES
HOUSE OF REPRESENTATIVES

ONE HUNDRED FIFTEENTH CONGRESS

FIRST SESSION

HEARING HELD
MARCH 29, 2017

U.S. GOVERNMENT PUBLISHING OFFICE

25–095   WASHINGTON : 2017

CONTENTS

Page

STATEMENTS PRESENTED BY MEMBERS OF CONGRESS

WITNESSES

APPENDIX

MILITARY PILOT SHORTAGE

House of Representatives,
Committee on Armed Services,
Subcommittee on Military Personnel,
Washington, DC, Wednesday, March 29, 2017.

The subcommittee met, pursuant to call, at 2:00 p.m., in room 2118, Rayburn House Office Building, Hon. Mike Coffman (chairman of the subcommittee) presiding.

OPENING STATEMENT OF HON. MIKE COFFMAN, A REPRESENTATIVE FROM COLORADO, CHAIRMAN, SUBCOMMITTEE ON MILITARY PERSONNEL

Mr. COFFMAN. The hearing comes to order. I want to welcome everyone to the Military Personnel Subcommittee hearing on the shortage of pilots in the military services. Today, we will hear from the services on their progress toward increasing the retention of military pilots, both officers and warrant officers.

We know that pilot demand is increasing in the commercial sector, and the demand to hire qualified military pilots is higher than the available pool of candidates. This demand has led to a shortage of pilots across the services, with the problem being particularly acute in the United States Air Force, with a deficit at this point of over 1,000 total pilots.

And we are here today to hear from the armed services on their plans to stem the exit of pilots from the military. We know we cannot buy our way out of this problem since the military cannot compete with the potential salaries and, in some cases, the lifestyle of the commercial airlines. So we must make sure the services are using all the levers in their control, from an increase in bonuses to changes in the assignment system to changes in promotion to incentives, these pilots—to incentivize these pilots to remain in the military.

The Military Personnel Subcommittee will take every opportunity to thoroughly review and discuss the way forward to stop the outflow of military pilots. I look forward to hearing from the witnesses to understand the scope of the pilot retention problem and to assess the proposed resolutions for the services in increasing retention.

Before I introduce our panel, let me offer Ranking Member Speier an opportunity to make opening remarks.

Representative Speier.

[The prepared statement of Mr. Coffman can be found in the Appendix on page 31.]

(1)

STATEMENT OF HON. JACKIE SPEIER, A REPRESENTATIVE FROM CALIFORNIA, RANKING MEMBER, SUBCOMMITTEE ON MILITARY PERSONNEL

Ms. SPEIER. Mr. Chairman, thank you. And thank you to our witnesses who are here today.

The Armed Services Committee has been receiving quite a bit of testimony over the last few months on the issue of readiness. There remains some debate on the severity of the readiness crisis or even whether it exists at all. For the most part, the solutions being considered by the administration and Congress involve vast funding increases so that the Department can buy new equipment and end strength.

The shortage of military pilots does, of course, have a direct impact on readiness. So the reaction to the shortage has typically been along the same veins: to throw more money at the problem in the form of cash retention bonuses. But without addressing the root causes, this will do little to stem the departure of valuable experienced military pilots.

As the witnesses and several members of the subcommittee are well aware, our service members are not in it for the money. Military pilots serve for love of country and for love of flying. There are many reasons besides money that military pilots leave the service for the private sector, including family concerns and a desire for more stability, too few flying hours, and too many assigned tasks unrelated to flying.

Today, I am interested in hearing how each of the services are working to identify these root causes and how you use that analysis and the authorities Congress has provided to better target nonmonetary incentives as well as monetary in order to increase retention. I am also interested to hear what joint initiatives you may be undertaking together across services.

It costs millions of dollars and years of training to produce just a single aviator. I am not telling you something you don't already know. We therefore need to ensure we are thinking broadly and creatively about how best to retain the skilled aviators the Nation needs.

Thank you, and I look forward to your testimony.

Mr. COFFMAN. Thank you, Ms. Speier.

We will give each witness the opportunity to present his or her testimony and each member an opportunity to question the witnesses for 5 minutes.

We would also respectfully remind the witnesses to summarize, to the greatest extent possible, the high points of your written testimony in 5 minutes or less. Your written comments and statements will be made part of the hearing record.

Let me welcome our panel: Lieutenant General Mark A. Brilakis, Deputy Commandant for Manpower and Reserve Affairs, United States Marine Corps; Vice Admiral Robert P. Burke, [Deputy] Chief of Naval Operations; Lieutenant General Gina M. Grosso, Deputy Chief of Staff for Manpower and Personnel Services, United States Air Force; Major General Erik C. Peterson, United States Army, Director, Army Aviation.

With that, General Brilakis, you are recognized for 5 minutes.

STATEMENT OF LTGEN MARK A. BRILAKIS, USMC, DEPUTY COMMANDANT FOR MANPOWER AND RESERVE AFFAIRS, UNITED STATES MARINE CORPS

General BRILAKIS. Thank you, Mr. Chairman.

Chairman Coffman, Ranking Member Speier, and distinguished members of the subcommittee, I appreciate the opportunity to appear before you today to provide an overview of the Marine Corps inventory of pilots and aviators. Since the first Marine aviator flew in 1912, our pilots, like all marines, have answered the Nation's call, faithfully serving the American people and maintaining a first-class standard of military excellence. Today, Marine aviation is providing critical support to combat operations, and the Marine Corps is and will continue to be our Nation's expeditionary force in readiness.

Aviators and our aviation maintenance personnel are critical to our ability to meet the continued and increasing operational commitments, operational tempo, and challenging deployment-to-dwell ratios.

While the Marine Corps does not currently have a shortage of aviation personnel, we are experiencing a shortage of trained aviators, particularly in specific platforms, and gaps in the necessary qualifications of our enlisted maintenance personnel. This is in large part exacerbated by current readiness issues with our aircraft. Addressing these issues is one of mine and the Deputy Commandant for Aviation's highest priorities.

Aviation readiness in the form of Ready Basic Aircraft and the resources to operate them throughout the year is the single most important factor in alleviating our aviation manpower challenges and contributing to retention. Our responsibility to train and to retain the best aviators and maintainers for our Corps is an operational imperative for us. We vigorously attack the accession and retention of all our Marine occupational fields, and doing so for the aviation field is particularly important due to the time and expense required to train these marines. We will continue to closely monitor the trends of our aviators, and we will take action should we begin to see a retention problem so that your Corps remains the most ready when the Nation is the least ready.

Thank you for the opportunity to present this testimony.

[The prepared statement of General Brilakis can be found in the Appendix on page 32.]

Mr. COFFMAN. Vice Admiral Burke, you are now recognized for 5 minutes.

STATEMENT OF VADM ROBERT P. BURKE, USN, CHIEF OF NAVAL PERSONNEL, UNITED STATES NAVY

Admiral BURKE. Thank you, Chairman Coffman, Ranking Member Speier, and distinguished members of the subcommittee for this opportunity to discuss the status of naval aviation retention. I am honored to represent the men and women of the United States Navy.

Naval aviation today is strong, the most capable maritime air force in the world, and our deployed units are ready to respond to any challenge. It is made up of more than 190,000 military and Navy civilian personnel, including 10,250 Navy pilots and naval flight officers, who safely and effectively maintain, operate, and train with approximately 3,700 aircraft in support of worldwide carrier-based and expeditionary missions, to include combat operations.

On any given day, two to five of our nine carrier air wings are deployed, returning from a deployment, or preparing to deploy. Our ability to sustain this effort depends upon a number of factors, among the most critical of which is our people. So I am here today to outline the current risks and projected manning challenges facing naval aviation and what we must do to sustain peak combat readiness. Our ability to attract and retain the very best young men and women our Nation has to offer is central to maintaining aviation personnel readiness.

A number of factors are making this challenge increasingly complex, including an improving economy with low unemployment and increasing opportunity for employment in the private sector, particularly within the commercial airline industry. Additionally, naval aviators have expressed dissatisfaction with the quality of service, resulting from readiness challenges associated with limited aircraft availability and reduced flying hours while not deployed, which have inhibited timely attainment of tactical qualifications and subsequent career progression.

Those who wear the cloth of this Nation do not do so for the money but rather to be part of something bigger than themselves. Historically, we have also been able to positively influence retention behavior by providing a fair compensation package, but more importantly, we provide an enticement few other employers can offer: a call to service.

However, the allure of service is diminished when readiness shortfalls inhibit sailors' ability to get the job done. Today, aviation depots struggle to get our airplanes through maintenance periods on time. These delays impact the time sailors have to train and hone their skills prior to deployment. Such challenges are further exacerbated by low stocks of critical spare parts and an aging shore infrastructure. While our first team on deployment is always ready, our bench, the depth of our forces at home, is thin and is growing increasingly frustrated. Additionally, operational tempo, uncertain deployment schedules, excessive administrative burdens, and quality-of-life issues for sailors' families, including late permanent change of station orders and limited housing options, especially in non-fleet concentration areas, adversely affect individuals' decisions to stay Navy.

Restoring short-term fleet readiness will require sufficient and predictable funding, which will allow our pilots to fly the hours needed to maintain optimum proficiency and ensure our ability to conduct timely maintenance on our airframes. It would also enable the Navy to restore stocks of necessary parts, return more aircraft to operational status, and better prepare them to remain deployed, as required. Finally, it would allow our pilots to do what they want to do, which is to fly.

We will continue to aggressively pursue resolution of aviator retention challenges through effective and responsible use of available resources and refinements to our plans and processes for recruiting, developing, retaining, and addressing the quality of service needs of our aviators.

We welcome your assistance, look forward to working with you to address the challenges we face, and we appreciate your continued support for initiatives designed to help us achieve optimum personnel readiness, improve quality of service, and retain the best and brightest young men and women this Nation has to offer. Thank you, and I look forward to your questions.

[The prepared statement of Admiral Burke can be found in the Appendix on page 38.]

Mr. COFFMAN. Thank you, Vice Admiral Burke.

Lieutenant General Grosso, you are now recognized for 5 minutes.

STATEMENT OF LT GEN GINA M. GROSSO, USAF, DEPUTY CHIEF OF STAFF FOR MANPOWER AND PERSONNEL SERVICES, UNITED STATES AIR FORCE

General GROSSO. Thank you, Chairman Coffman, Ranking Member Speier, and distinguished members of the subcommittee for the opportunity to discuss the status of the Air Force pilot shortages and our efforts to address it.

America's Air Force has been globally engaged for the last 26 years in combat operations. During that time, we have provided air dominance through global vigilance, global reach, and global power for our joint force. Make no mistake: your Air Force is always there.

However, being always there comes at a cost to equipment, infrastructure, and, most importantly, our airmen. And we are now at a decision point. Sustained global commitments and recent funding cuts affect capacity and capability for a full-spectrum fight against a near-peer adversary. Compounding this issue, an upcoming surge of mandatory retirements for airline pilots and an increasing market for global commerce is causing the civilian aviation industry to begin hiring at unprecedented rates.

This confluence of circumstances has birthed a national aircrew crisis. This crisis is the result of multiple factors: high operational tempo over the last 26 years, a demand for our pilots from the commercial industry, and cultural issues that affect the quality of life and service for our airmen.

As we closed fiscal year 2016, the total force, including our Active, Guard, and Reserve Components, was short 1,555 pilots across all mission areas. Of this amount, the total force was short 1,211 fighter pilots. It should be noted that the cost to train a fifth-generation fighter pilot to prepare him or her for their first operational squadron is approximately $11 million. A 1,200 fighter pilot shortage amounts to a $12 billion capital loss for the United States Air Force.

Civilian aviation companies are actively recruiting the world-class experience of our rated airmen because Air Force pilots are highly attractive with their diverse experience and quality aviation training. Outpacing RAND's 2016 study, major airlines hired more than 4,100 pilots last year, and they increased the salary of their pilot force by an average of 17 percent. These annual hiring levels are expected to continue for the next 10 to 15 years.

Civilian job prospects are not the sole reason the Air Force is losing talent. A 2015 exit survey revealed additional influences to leave include too many duties unrelated to flying, inability to maintain work-life balance, and availability of civilian jobs, in that order.

The Air Force's plan to address these shortfalls is three-pronged: reduce requirements, increase production, and increase retention. The Air Force reduced the number of pilots filling operational planning positions in order to prioritize manning at flying squadrons. We also are leveraging our total force partners to bolster staff and operational planning positions, deployments, and in pilot training units, as appropriate.

The Air Force recognizes the need to increase pilot production and will expand undergraduate pilot training to maximum capacity at 1,400 pilots a year. Future increases in throughput will require additional manpower, infrastructure, operations, and maintenance resources.

From a retention perspective, the Air Force is implementing many nonmonetary programs to strengthen the culture and improve the quality of life and service for our airmen. For example, we reduced additional duties, eliminated non-mission-essential training courses, and outsourced select routine administrative tasks and operational squadrons, just to name a few. All of these efforts give time back to our aviators so they can focus on their primary duty: flying.

We are also grateful for your support to authorize an increase in the aviation bonus to $35,000 a year, the first increase in 18 years. Through a tiered business case analysis, we will identify areas of greatest need to retain pilots in exchange for a commitment beyond their initial service commitment. We are also considering incentives for hard-to-fill assignments, when many airmen choose to separate from service in lieu of accepting the assignment.

The Air Force is committed to a holistic strategy to maintain our pilot inventory as we face external and internal challenges. While we aggressively pursue creative means to respond to the demands on our pilots, our attention will be focused on developing an agile set of solutions. We will not hesitate to seek your support for revised or new authorities and resources, as appropriate. We appreciate your support as we address the competition for our talented aviators and move out on bold and innovative solutions.

Thank you for your time today on this important matter. I look forward to your questions.

[The prepared statement of General Grosso can be found in the Appendix on page 46.]

Mr. COFFMAN. Lieutenant General Grosso, thank you so much for your testimony.

Major General Peterson, you are now recognized for 5 minutes.

STATEMENT OF MG ERIK C. PETERSON, USA, DIRECTOR, ARMY AVIATION, UNITED STATES ARMY

General PETERSON. Chairman Coffman, Ranking Member Speier, and distinguished members of the subcommittee, I appreciate the opportunity to discuss Army Aviation pilot shortages and our mitigation strategy.

Army Aviation is an asymmetric advantage for our joint air-ground team, providing the reach, protection, lethality, and situational understanding required to win. At the foundation are our highly trained Army Aviation professionals. The pilot component of our Total Army aviation force consists of 14,000 rated aviators across the Regular Army, the Army National Guard, and the Army Reserve.

Several years of sustained fiscal constraints have required the Army to make difficult resourcing choices. Out of necessity, we have prioritized short-term readiness over long-term recruiting and training. We simply could not afford to train the number of new pilots we need to sustain a healthy force, a growing challenge that is masked by relatively healthy current aggregate strength. Specifically, we have accumulated a shortage of 731 Regular Army aviation warrant officers across year groups 2010 through 2017. We are temporarily sustaining acceptable aggregate pilot manning by relying on senior aviation warrant officers to fill junior positions, over 25 percent of which are retirement eligible.

We are addressing these challenges and we will build long-term readiness through three lines of effort: retention, training throughput, and accessions. Retention of experienced pilots is key to mitigating 7 years of constrained training throughput. Although overall Army retention is healthy, we have seen a recent increase in Army Aviation warrant officer attrition from 7 to 9 percent annually. Given growing commercial demand, we expect this trend to continue unless addressed.

In anticipation, we are formalizing targeted incentives that encourage pilots to continue their Army aviation careers and to retain those who achieve advanced qualifications. Additionally, we are correcting the accumulated deficit in our training throughput by fully resourcing our flight school. Fully resourcing our flight school is not a quick fix, and it must be phased in over several years. It will require consistent funding at increased levels to be successful. We are also increasing our aviation warrant officer accessions in concert with the increased throughput of our pilot training. Over the next 3 years, we will increase our Regular Army aviation warrant officer accession training throughput by nearly 170 students annually.

In summary, we are addressing our pilot manning challenges while simultaneously meeting our enduring requirements. We currently have the sufficient authorities to implement our pilot retention, training throughput, and accessions increase. However, sustained, predictable, on-time funding, and relief from the Budget Control Act are vital to any enduring solution that we attempt to apply.

Mr. Chairman, Ranking Member, distinguished members of the committee, thank you for your enduring support of our Army and your shared commitment to our Nation's defense.

[The prepared statement of General Peterson can be found in the Appendix on page 58.]

Mr. COFFMAN. Thank you, Major General Peterson. I wish to thank—oh. I won't do that again.

So, if we look at the biggest reason on the demand side of this equation, I think it is two factors, and I don't know which one is dominant. So one factor is you have got an aging population of pilots on the civil aviation side, and that might have been aggravated by the fact that they increased the retirement age for pilots and so—and now we are hitting that increased retirement age. And so we are seeing some significant retirements. So that is obviously part of the demand side. But a significant part of the demand side too, I would think, is that, in response to an aviation accident—I am trying to remember what year it was. I think it was in New York State.

General GROSSO. 2012, I think.

Mr. COFFMAN. 2012? There were—the reaction to that was to plus-up the number of hours required to, I believe, 1,500 flight hours——

General GROSSO. Yes, sir.

Mr. COFFMAN [continuing]. For the civilian airlines, FAA [Federal Aviation Administration] requirement. And so the quickest way to get that is to look at the military, because that is very hard to get on the civilian side. And so—and I don't know if that—if the FAA needs to revisit that number, if that was an overreaction to that accident or not, but that does seem excessive. So that is on the demand side.

And then—so, on the supply side, I believe, I know, Lieutenant General Grosso, you briefed me on a retention bonus structure that you want to put forward. Do you want to tell the subcommittee about that? And before you do, let me just preface it by saying that I really think that, within the National Defense Authorization Act [NDAA], there really needs to be an econometric reevaluation of that number on an annual basis that will adjust accordingly. This situation is not going to last forever. It is demand-and-supply curve, and eventually that demand is going to be satiated at some level.

General Grosso.

General GROSSO. Thank you, Chairman Coffman.

Sir, you are correct. In accordance with the guidance we received in the 2017 authorization act, we did come up with a business model to understand where our greatest need was. And this model is the model we use to give all special and incentive pays across every skill set in the Air Force, which is about $927 million across the Air Force, but it has four factors: manning, retention, replacement costs, and replacement time. And manning is weighted at 40 percent, retention at 40 percent, replacement cost at 10 percent, and replacement time at 10 percent. And basically you put all these numbers together, and you get rank ordering. And based on the increase in the bonus, which you gave us in the 2017 NDAA as well, we looked at the greatest need, and we stair-stepped it down to match the weapons systems that were most in need in accordance with your direction.

And we will do this every single year. So the program we come out with this year could look different than the program we come out with next year because, to your point, the environment may change, and people that choose to come and go will change.

Mr. COFFMAN. Is the bonus structure the same across the board? Are you—do you mirror the Air Force, or do you all have your own structure that you are looking at?

General Brilakis.

General BRILAKIS. Sir, thank you.

And, first of all, thank you to the Congress for the authorities in the NDAA.

Since 2011, the Marine Corps has not paid a retention bonus to pilots. Our inventories were solid, and attrition was not a challenge.

Now, what we did, we came down from 202,000, and we have arrived at 182,000. In doing that, in leveraging all the authorities that you gave us, the priority was to reduce numbers of marines. And we saw an unequal reduction. And our retention, which is ideally about 91 percent for aviators, in the officer community, fell down to 86 and 87 percent. So we lost some aviators. We have made that up through accessions. And our challenge right now is I have got about 500, just over 500 officers still in the training pipeline, more than I need.

Mr. COFFMAN. Okay.

General BRILAKIS. Okay? This year, the Commandant, because, in addition to reducing the size of the force, we are introducing new type/model/series into the inventory, the F–35, we are continuing the MV–22, the new versions of the Cobra and Huey, et cetera, the Commandant is going forward requesting from the Secretary of the Navy and the Secretary of Defense authority to pay a retention bonus in three communities: F–35; F–18, because the legacy platforms are our most challenged platform right now; and then the V–22. F–35 and V–22 are currently growing communities, and we don't want to be caught short in those aviation communities.

When we came down in the reduction, what we found is we are a bit imbalanced. We have got more majors and lieutenant colonels than is preferred. We have fewer company-grade officers than we really need to be flying in our tactical squadrons. And so we want to make sure that we have the opportunity and leverage to maintain those young officers as they come out of their required commitment to us and capture them for that extra bit of time before we have got them by the throat.

Mr. COFFMAN. Thank you, General Brilakis.

Ms. Speier, you are now recognized.

Ms. SPEIER. Thank you, Mr. Chairman.

Thank you all for your service to our country. General Grosso, the $35,000 bonus, I am presuming that that is not going to be a check that is presented to the airman on day one.

General GROSSO. That is correct, ma'am. Aviators in the Air Force have a 10-year pilot service commitment. So that is when they graduate from the undergraduate pilot training. So that training takes a year, and after that year, they have a 10-year commitment. So it is typically at the 11th year of service that an airman would be offered some form of bonus should we need it.

Ms. SPEIER. But is that $35,000 given in a lump sum, or is it given per year based on the number of years that the aviator would continue to serve?

General GROSSO. So it can be a range of options. And every year we look at this differently. This year we are proposing to offer contracts for a year, 2 years, 5 years, 9 years, and 13 years, and you can take some of that up front, and some of it will be anniversary payments.

Ms. SPEIER. So no one aviator is going to get a $35,000 check, or will they?

General GROSSO. It would—if they took it for a year, yes, ma'am, they would. And they would—they would owe us an additional year Active Duty service commitment.

Ms. SPEIER. So, conceivably, an aviator would stay a total of 2 years and get a $35,000 bonus in day one? What happens if they decide to just quit? Do you claw that back?

General GROSSO. Yes, ma'am. Yes. You must recoup. And the thinking on the 1 year was because of the work that we are doing on the culture piece, those things take time. And we have to build trust with our airmen, because after significant long periods of conflict where we took our eye off the ball a little bit, we have talked about putting resources back in the squadron. One of our chief's primary goals is to revitalize the squadron, and we think that is getting traction, but that will take time. And we have gotten feedback from airmen they—if they—they are going to give us a year, basically. So they are going to take it for a year and see if we really mean what we say with some of these quality of life and quality of service, and then that gives them a chance to relook and take— in another year say, "Hey, are we doing better? Is my family in a good place? Did you do what you say you are going to, Air Force?" And then, next year, they will go into a new—we will look at the environment; we will look at what our retention patterns look like.

Ms. SPEIER. Okay. I am trying to get another question in.

I particularly wanted to talk about nonmonetary inducements. And I noted that, in the report, there was a reference made to 260 days away during deployment for some of these aviators and 110 days away even when you are on home temporary duty. So those are long stretches away. And in your actual statement, General Grosso, there is a chart here that shows that actually the ranking of the lure of civilian jobs is much lower than additional duties, which was at 37 percent, and maintaining work-life balance and meeting family commitments, which was at 31 percent. Availability of civilian jobs was at 24 percent.

So I think the lure of commercial airline jobs, while it does have some allure, I think addressing those top two would be significant. So, to each of you, I would like to ask the question in a minute 36, what, if anything, you are doing to try and address the nonmonetary issues.

General BRILAKIS. Thank you, Ranking Member Speier.

We did a survey about 18 months ago, and talking to our enlisted force and our officers on those issues of most importance to them. Flying hours is the number one concern. They want more time in the cockpit. They want more time in the back. Number two was the parts available to get those aircraft up so they could do that flying. And then the last—the third issue, which was of most concern to them, was the cycle, the tight cycle. As you know, the Marine Corps is on about a 1-to-2 ratio for deployment to dwell, and that is a very tight cycle. So three concerns: one, they want more time to fly; they want more parts to fix; and they would like a little bit more time at home.

Ms. SPEIER. Okay. Admiral Burke.

Admiral BURKE. Yes, ma'am. Similar situation for the Navy as the Marine Corps. It is flying time first. Again, they are getting plenty of it while they are deployed. Our deployment lengths had ramped up considerably as our force size went down over the course of 15 years, while our, you know, number of ships at sea on any given day remained the same. That is starting to come under control now.

The things like PCS [permanent change of station] move lead times shrank down as we used PCS funding as a means of making our top-line budget come within under control. So families were getting a month, month and a half of lead time to move in the summer going to non-fleet concentration areas where it was difficult to find housing and things of that nature.

And then just other sort of normal quality-of-service types of things, administrative distractions, career flexibility. We have really been using the tremendous flexibility that you gave us with the Career Intermission Program to good effect, particularly in the aviation community. We have had 13 aviators in, and 9 have come through it. In fact——

Ms. SPEIER. Okay. My time has expired. Let's see if we can——

Mr. COFFMAN. Go ahead.

Admiral BURKE. Sir, we just had a female O–4, was one of our top helicopters pilots that would have gotten out. We were able to convince her to take advantage of the Career Intermission Program so that she could get out. She was married to a naval aviator as well. And she got out, started a family. Just finished her intermission. Came back in, did her department head tour, did absolutely phenomenally, last week screened for commanding officer. So another success story there.

But it is things like that where we have to add the career flexibility while our pilots are out of the cockpit to do life things and come back in and reenter the cockpit and be competitive in their careers.

Mr. COFFMAN. Mr. Russell, you are now recognized for 5 minutes.

General GROSSO. Ma'am, we also have done—I would put it——

Ms. SPEIER. Actually, maybe you could fold your answers into responses.

Mr. COFFMAN. We can come back to that.

Ms. SPEIER. Oh. We will come back to that question.

Mr. COFFMAN. Mr. Russell, you are recognized for 5 minutes.

Mr. RUSSELL. Thank you, Mr. Chairman.

And I appreciate all of the things that you do. A couple of the questions—it is bonus question time. How much does American Airlines offer bonuses up to their pilots, for regional pilots? Bueller? Anyone? It is $35,000. Interesting figure.

And so, you know, once again, we go in this chasing around that the $35,000 is some astronomical figure, when the reality is that is competitive to what the airlines are providing to very junior pilots in the course of their careers. And, you know, the phrase that comes to mind is nothing's too good for the troops, and nothing's what they get, you know.

So I applaud, you General Grosso, for putting together the pro-posals for the bonuses. They do retain.

And, General Peterson, if I may, because of your extensive back-ground in 160th SOAR [Special Operations Aviation Regiment], you are a very unique pilot with a very unique background. If you don't have the types of pilots in our special ops aviation commu-nity, what impact does that have on the missions that our Rangers and our special operations forces [SOF] community do that we rely so heavily on for most of our missions? Could you speak to that for a little bit?

General PETERSON. Without the retention of hand-selected and then exceptionally highly trained aircraft commanders, pilots, and command—air mission commanders, one, we would not be able to accomplish the complex missions in support of our elite SOF ground forces that our Nation asks us to do. The physical skill, the planning ability, the judgment, the maturity, and the leadership would not be present, and we would not have the ability to accu-mulate and grow that in support of the missions that they are asked for.

Further, we would not be able to sustain those capabilities over time. Those same leaders that are selected and are retained at some cost and investment are also the mentors and teachers for the next generation. So they serve to accomplish their missions today, but they also grow the next generation that our Nation will rely upon.

Mr. RUSSELL. Well, I can tell you from my own experiences, even as a combat infantryman, without helicopters to have conveyed us to a location, we would have had a lot less options on how to get to the enemy. And even without the United States Air Force, our paratroopers would have no delivery capability of any length to get to or even logistics or emergency supply parts or any number of things.

So, really, this pilot shortage goes beyond just having, you know, somebody with the flight suit and standing next to the aircraft with a cool picture. It literally is everything that our military relies on no matter what their capacity is. And yet a typical warrant—you are talking about the aging of the warrant population. Even a W4, what are they making? $60,000 a year? I am not sure what it would be today. Anybody have an idea of what that would be?

General PETERSON. It would be closer to $80,000 a year.

Mr. RUSSELL. 80? Okay. So $80,000. And yet it takes $11 million to train a pilot to their first combat mission. Now, you know, I am not a mathematics major or a rocket scientist, but, you know, $11 million or $35,000. Let's see, retain them a couple more years or not. It seems like a good investment because when we don't do it, much like the cliff that we had with our air traffic controllers in the 1980s, when President Reagan said, "Okay, fine, you want to protest; we will just hire a bunch of new ones," and they did, but then they all left in one shot. And 25 percent of the pilot force just in the Army, not only are you losing your most experienced war-riors as they go out of the cockpits and out of the service, but you don't readily replace them, and then you are not going to have the incentive to bring them in.

And so I just want to say, for the record, I applaud what you do. We have to fix the problem. We can't ignore it and we can't say: "Hey, you know, we will give you some busted up, you know, Army relief service furniture or something in your quarters, and that will be a good incentive for you." We have to do better.

So, with that, I am out of time. And thank you, Mr. Chairman.

Mr. COFFMAN. Thank you, Mr. Russell.

Mr. Gallego, you are now recognized for 5 minutes.

Mr. GALLEGO. Thank you, Mr. Chairman.

This is really for all the witnesses. So better data is obviously critical in shaping the response to the emerging pilot shortage we have in the military. Have we undertaken a comprehensive survey to better understand the pilot attitudes, whether it is across the services or each individual services or within each individual MOS [military occupational specialty], or whatever it is called on the officer level, and the factors that drive their decisions to either renew their commitments to serve or to pursue other careers with commercial airlines or just outside the military altogether?

And we can just start from left to right with Lieutenant General Brilakis.

General BRILAKIS. Thank you very much, Representative Gallego.

As I said earlier, about 18 months ago, we pursued a specific survey to take a look at both officer and enlisted attitudes. We got good information from that. We are working on a longitudinal set of surveys that will cover a marine either from their first enlist- ment all the way through a 30-year career. It allows us to go in and take a look at attitudes on retention and separation, et cetera. So we believe that that will provide us better information in the future.

The specific targeted survey that we did gave us really great feedback. It is not about money. It is not necessarily about jobs. It is about doing what they came into the Marine Corps to do, which is to fly airplanes, fix airplanes, and then serve those aircraft.

On the officer side, our challenge is the number of Ready Basic Aircraft. It has been an issue. We have worked hard through it. And having those aircraft available to get that flight time, get the marine—get the pilots those hours per month that are necessary. On the enlisted side, it is the same thing. It is the satisfaction of seeing an aircraft you are responsible for actually take off loaded with bombs to go do the mission. And so those are the things we are working on as well.

On our enlisted side, we are looking at—we do bonus for retention, but we are also looking to—seeking to capture experience, to retain it into—in the squadrons, and that is another initiative we are bringing forward this year.

But you are absolutely right. Data is important. And we have specific data for right now, but we are working on having better data for the future.

Mr. GALLEGO. Thank you.

Admiral BURKE. Yes, sir. We do the exact same approach in the Navy, looking at everything from things that will inform our entire portfolio of Sailor 2025 efforts, which is aimed at everything under the nonmonetary aspect of things, everything from how we do detailing and assignments processes, to evaluations and fitness reports, to promotion boards and promotion policies, all the way down to, you know, our physical fitness programs and health and wellness things.

But in addition to looking at all that data and our family services and spousal employment and all those sorts of aspects, I mean, we have a very good pulse on exactly where we stand with retention at our critical points. We target our retention bonuses for our naval aviators at the two critical points, which are department head, which is at the lieutenant commander level for naval aviators, and then at the post-command level after they have had O–5 or commander command. And we vary the rate at which we pay the bonuses by the type, model, and series of aircraft. And that is really largely a reflection of what their opportunities, how their job skills might translate into the outside job markets.

And we know exactly how many have committed, because the contract lengths are designed to obligate them through that critical career milestone. So we have a very good indicator at all times of how many we have committed. And we talk to them almost on a weekly basis, how many are on the fence, how many are likely to say yes, and how many are definitely going to say no. So we keep a pulse of that all the time, and that helps inform our force management, if that answers your question.

General GROSSO. We do, sir. We have—there is a survey you will see in the written statement, which is a retention survey that goes to the entire force every other year, and that is the data that Ranking Member Speier pointed out. But we also have exit surveys, and an exit survey is a person that has told us they are going to leave. They have established what we call the date of separation. And so that gives you sort of more real-time thinking.

And that—from our pilots, the data is about the same. Maintaining work-life balance is the number one reason, and that is 45 percent. Availability of civilian jobs is 28 percent. And the potential to leave your family. And if you think about an aviator, over their 12 years of commitment, in a 1-to-3 dwell, every 3 years, they have deployed 180 days. And they come back, because they are not proficient in the high-end fight, they go on TDY [temporary duty] a lot to get proficient again. So, when you are forcing the—sort of looking at their options, in the structure of the civilian airline industry, there is an incentive to get in early. So I realize I am out of time, but——

Mr. COFFMAN. Go ahead, please, General Grosso. Go ahead and finish.

General GROSSO. So the way the civilian industry is structured, it is a sort of first-in/move-up system. So, as you are at the 12-year point and you are looking back on a very busy life and things that we need do better on quality of service, which we are looking on, they say, "Gosh, should I get out and start my line number"—many of them affiliate in the Reserve Component—so that they can start that successful second career for their family. And that is why that 12-year point is very important from a civilian hiring. And we know, we have data going back 30 years, that as airline hiring goes up, retention goes down, and we can correlate that.

Mr. COFFMAN. Mr. Bacon, you are now recognized for 5 minutes.

Mr. BACON. Thank you, Mr. Chairman.

I appreciate all four of you being here today again for subcommittee. Grateful to you.

What I would like to ask those who are doing the bonus, do we have some data that shows that it is actually effective, that it is a good return on investment, because we know how many people sign up for the bonus, but how do we know how many of those would have signed up anyway to stay in? Do we have some data that shows that this does bring a sizeable number over?

And the genesis of my concern is a lot of the reasons people are getting out has very little to do with the money itself; it is more about the other factors that were mentioned here. So just curious, can we correlate the number of folks that take the bonus by percentage or that said that that was the main reason why they stayed in?

General GROSSO. I can't correlate it that way, but what I can tell you, we did look· people that don't take the bonus, 96 percent separate. So we do know that people that don't take the bonus separate, and we do know that about two·thirds of them go to the airlines. So one·third don't.

But to your point, there is no question that you are paying some people to stay. So we think—I think all of us would agree, one·third, one·third, one·third, but because it is such a precious resource and because we invest so much money to make them, we think the tradeoff is worth it.

Mr. BACON. But we are not really too sure how many of those who sign up for the bonus would have stayed in anyway.

General GROSSO. No. You are correct.

Mr. BACON. Okay.

Admiral BURKE. Similar situation for the Navy. You just—you get to the point where, for some individuals, it could be economic, right. Exactly right.

General PETERSON. With respect to the Army, sir, we are not applying the bonus at this point to our overall forces. We have used it as a targeted incentive in our special operations community only. And we feel like we have very good return on investment and trends with that very small population, but we are anticipating employing some of these incentives beginning in fiscal year 2018.

Mr. BACON. Okay. And I know you are not doing the bonus, I don't believe, on the Marine side, right?

General BRILAKIS. No, sir. This year for—in fiscal year 2018, we will, for the first time since 2011, we will offer a retention bonus in three communities, because those are the communities where we believe we have some concerns.

But to your point, statistically, analytically, et cetera, there is really not a whole lot of connection between paying a bonus and guaranteeing retention.

Mr. BACON. It seems to me that we could get that data with a little bit of research and asking the right questions, because I think it would help make the case better that this is a good investment, seeing direct correlation of more people signing up. Just my thoughts.

Thanks, Mr. Chairman. I yield back.

Mr. COFFMAN. Thank you, Mr. Bacon.

Let's see. Mr. Abraham, you are now recognized for 5 minutes.

Dr. ABRAHAM. Thank you, Mr. Chairman.

By trade, I am a physician, and when I refer a patient to a heart surgeon, I hopefully always send them to the best, because they actually hold a life in their hands, much as your aviators do. The difference is they also hold the life in their hand while, by the way, dodging bullets. So it is a whole different dynamic on the level of our—not only our military aviators, but our military personnel in all.

The other aspect is the intellectual knowledge base of an aviator that has been in service for 10 to 11 years is phenomenal, and I would compare that to a top tier executive level in a company as IBM, one of the big ones. And when they give them bonuses, they are not talking thousands; they are talking millions of retention bonuses to keep that intellectual property in place.

Major General Peterson, I will ask you the question first. How does a CR [continuing resolution] for the remainder of fiscal year 2017 affect pilot shortage?

General PETERSON. In the very straight, simple terms, sir, it stops our initiatives to mitigate this. We will not be able to increase the throughput in our flight school with respect to investments in additional instructor pilots, contract instructor pilots, contract maintenance, as well as sustained additional airframes for the school. So it will essentially defer this problem another year until we have the requisite funding that has been budgeted for by the Army to implement these incentives. And then we will get closer to that cliff that we discussed about with the top-heavy population, the disproportionate top-heavy retirement eligible population.

Dr. ABRAHAM. If we carry that forward with an imposition of sequestration in 2018, what does that do for your readiness?

General Peterson, I will start with you.

General PETERSON. In addition to exacerbating the pilot readiness challenge that we have, we will suffer readiness hurdles. With respect to airframe material readiness, very significant and important modernization programs will either be halted or slowed, to include the CH–47 Block 2, the Improved Turbine Engine Program, the Future Vertical Lift initiative and program. Probably the most salient and important is that we will slow or defer very important protection and countermeasures initiatives that are underway right now.

Dr. ABRAHAM. Other comments on the CR 2017, how will it affect each of y'all's services? If you don't mind going down the line.

General BRILAKIS. Sir, if I—yeah. Real quickly, sir, very similar to General Peterson. We won't be able to execute the bonuses that we would like to. Our retention season actually begins in July. So that will be impacted. The funds that are available to do that won't be available. We will by the summertime have to basically idle 24 flying squadrons.

Dr. ABRAHAM. Wow.

General BRILAKIS. And then on top of that, with the lack of spares and repair parts, we are going to take a step backwards on the readiness efforts that we have done to bring back the number of Ready Basic Aircraft that are available for our pilots to fly.

Dr. ABRAHAM. Admiral Burke.

Admiral BURKE. For the Navy, we would be forced to reduce flight hours across all Navy aviation; 15 to 20 percent reduction in fleet replacement training squadrons. Those are the training squadrons. One-third of our junior aviators would not be able to complete basic qualifications and certifications. So squadrons going forward would be 20 to 30 percent undermanned, and that would pay forward for several years. I would be forced to cut accessions by a thousand going forward in April. That would translate directly to gapped billets at sea and ashore, including ultimately pilots, instructors, and aviation maintenance folks. And then there would be impacts to PCS fundings, which would cause delays in issuing orders and quality of service and quality of life, as we have discussed earlier. And then, similar to what General Brilakis laid out, we would have to stop bonus payments on most critical skills. So it would impact retention of, you know, experienced and specialized sailors, including aviation officers and aviation maintenance rates.

Dr. ABRAHAM. General, real quick.

General GROSSO. I echo—I mean, very much like the other services, it would have a devastating impact on our readiness, and we would have to stop flying, which has all the other negative consequences of trying to keep these aviators in the force.

Dr. ABRAHAM. Thank you, Mr. Chairman.

Well, just one comment. You know, it is my understanding that now it is difficult not only to maintain just currency but certainly to maintain readiness. And those are two different numbers of flight hours, I understand that; to be able to just to fly the plane but to be able to fly and fight are two completely separate and distinct issues.

Thank you, Mr. Chairman, for the indulgence.

Mr. COFFMAN. Dr. Wenstrup, you are now recognized for 5 minutes.

Dr. WENSTRUP. Thank you, Mr. Chairman. Thank you all for being here today.

One question. What is tougher right now, recruitment, initial recruitment, or retention? What do you have the most trouble with? If we can go down the line.

General BRILAKIS. Sir, fortunately, neither is a problem.

Admiral BURKE. Navy overall recruiting is good. We just made our 120th consecutive month of meeting our recruiting mission. We are seeing beginnings of fraying at the edges.

Overall, retention is good, although we are seeing individual specific areas, such as aviation officers, nuclear rates, special operations forces, and information warfare, you know, cryptological types of rates—we are having individual retention challenges there, but we are able to manage those with the authorities we have right now.

General GROSSO. We have no issue recruiting talented people to be aviators. Our sole issue is retention, and we are not retaining enough to sustain the force.

General PETERSON. We are not facing challenges with recruiting either. However, that recruiting pool is artificially restrained because of our throughput challenges due to tough fiscal decisions. We are seeing leading indicators of impending retention challenges

based on the retirement eligibility of our force as well as the increase in commercial demand.

Dr. WENSTRUP. And I just have another point of curiosity, I
guess. You are getting exit information, exit surveys. On the exit
survey, do you ask them why they joined to begin with, or do you
know that on entry? I imagine the entry reason is pretty much the
same for everybody, to be honest with you, for many reasons, want-
ing to serve, et cetera, but on their exit, do you ask them why they
joined? And I am just curious what changed for them to want to
leave.

General BRILAKIS. So what our experience—I commanded the recruiting force for a couple of years. So we had the opportunity to
kind of watch that. And you are right. I mean, the American youth
join the service in general for a number of predictable reasons.
Why they join each different service, again, some predictable reasons.

Why they leave, sometimes it is the opportunity to remain in the
Marine Corps. We only retain about 27 percent of every year's co-
hort because two-thirds of our force is in the operating forces and
about one-third is in the supporting establishment. And it is a
young force; it is a fighting force.

When I answered your question, I was talking about the aviation
enterprise, aviation maintainers, et cetera. We have some retention
issues in the cyber force and some of the high-demand, low-density
MOSes. Some of the reasons folks leave those is because there are
opportunities on the outside. I mean, I can take a cyber marine
who is getting paid maybe $55,000 a year; he is leaving and pick-
ing up a job for about $190,000 plus. Those are challenges that—
I don't think you are going to give us enough money to throw at
those particular problems, but why they come and why they go
have been pretty much standard across the board. The thing that
is amazing right now is, with the employment rate as low as it is,
we are still finding good people who want to serve.

Dr. WENSTRUP. That is good to hear. Good Americans. I am refer-
ring more to aviation than anything else. Admiral.

Admiral BURKE. I think a lot of people—well, now that you have
changed the question to be specific to aviation, I mean, they join
for the adventure and to be that part of something bigger than
themselves. And I think they find that here and they are generally
very happy with it.

Why they leave, I mean, all the reasons we talked about earlier,
but then there is the family separation thing. We ask a lot of our
folks, and it is not for everyone.

Dr. WENSTRUP. I am guessing a lot, when they enter, are young-
er, for one, and possibly single at the time.

Admiral BURKE. They grow up and mature, and things change.

Dr. WENSTRUP. Yeah. General.

General GROSSO. Yes, I would agree with that. They are just at
different points in their life. And I think you make decisions de-
pending on your situation 12 years later, which is very different
than when you joined.

Dr. WENSTRUP. Right.

General PETERSON. Although I can presume that trends are probably the same, I am not aware of any specific question that we are asking on an exit survey that would substantiate that.

Dr. WENSTRUP. All right. Thank you. I yield back.

Mr. COFFMAN. Mr. Kelly, you are now recognized for 5 minutes.

Mr. KELLY. Thank you, Mr. Chairman.

And, General Peterson, I am going to start with you real quick and talk about ARI [Aviation Restructure Initiative]. And they asked about—or they were going to get UH–72 Lakotas to modernize and enhance pilot training at Fort Rucker, where they train our aviation pilots in the Army. The goal was to retire the older fleet and create a more relevant, safer, and cost-effective training. Could you update us on how the modernization of helicopter pilot training is progressing, to include observations from the initial pilot training classes on the Lakota trainer?

General PETERSON. Our modernization efforts are slowed a bit right now, just partially due to fiscal decisions on our fielding plans for the Lakota as well as some ongoing litigation.

The Lakota is proving to be an exceptionally reliable and very beneficial trainer. It is too early to comprehensively substantiate the full benefit.

What we do know is that the use of a more complex aircraft in initial pilot training, a twin-engine aircraft with essentially a modern glass cockpit, is translating very well to the assimilation of skills in the combat aircraft that the initial-entry aviators transition into for their subsequent training phases. And we are looking forward to substantiating that and objectively documenting that as we get to the pure fleet.

At this point, we are roughly half-and-half, with respect to the very early phases, with our legacy fleet training aircraft and the Lakota.

Mr. KELLY. And we have talked about—I am not going to put you on the spot, but the bottom line is there is a lawsuit that is slowing that down. And that definitely has an impact on not going forward and replacing with something, that has an impact on our training and readiness and the ability to train our new pilots.

Would that be correct, General Peterson?

General PETERSON. It does. But, again, we are compensating with the extension of the legacy aircraft, which was proven in past years, sir.

Mr. KELLY. And this is for Lieutenant General Grosso.

One question that I have, the $35,000 bonus, it amazes me that anyone questions that. After 5 years in service, that 11-year captain that gets out or a warrant officer, that 11-year person at that time that is critical, when they go to the airlines 5 years later, they are probably at the airline making double what a U.S. Army major or a U.S. Air Force major or a WO3 would be making at that point. Would be that correct?

General GROSSO. The data we have right now is very quickly you will get to $160,000 a year, so probably. I haven't really done the math, but I think that is correct.

Mr. KELLY. Yeah, quite a bit. And that is not for the 20-year guys. I know. I have missed every bonus I have ever been offered because I was too old to get it and been in too long when it became critical. But that is those 11- and 12-year people at that critical stage, that midlevel management, that is when that $35,000 is applied, that critical point in their career. Is that correct?

General GROSSO. That is correct.

Mr. KELLY. And this is for all three of you all. And I don't know if you have experienced it, but there are some things you can't replicate—you know, the CTCs [Combat Training Centers] in the military and the Army or your Red Flags in the Air Force or those things. But does anything replicate combat experience other than combat experience?

General BRILAKIS. I think it is relative to the combat experience you have gotten. If you are doing low-level counterinsurgency operation, you are getting a much better overall training experience at Red Flag or at the Fighter Weapons School or at WTI [Weapons and Tactics Instructor]. That is all high-end stuff against simulated high-threat IADS [integrated air defense systems]. But, I mean, combat is combat.

Mr. KELLY. And, again, those things are great, and I have done many of those things, but it still doesn't replicate.

And then I guess the final question that I would have is, it is not just the flying experience that you lose, it is also that command experience, that leadership, that management. So a brand-new flight trainee coming out of Columbus Air Force Base in my district does not have the same skills as that major who has been an operations officer for a squadron.

Would that be correct, Lieutenant General Grosso?

General GROSSO. Yes, sir, it would.

Mr. KELLY. And so, just taking out the flying side of that, you can't replicate that leadership experience at those critical levels, midlevel management, whether you are talking about maintenance in the NCO [noncommissioned officer] level or warrant officers who were WO3s or majors or senior captains. You can't replicate that anywhere, can you?

General GROSSO. No, you can't. It takes 10 years to make it.

Mr. KELLY. And if you get out, you can't get back in and start over at the same spot, can you?

General GROSSO. Well, we do have programs to bring people in that have separated. But it is challenging because we don't have enough capacity to train them again.

Mr. KELLY. Yes, ma'am. I yield back, Mr. Chairman.

Mr. COFFMAN. Thank you, Mr. Kelly.

Let's see. Colonel Martha McSally, United States Air Force, retired A–10 pilot, you are now recognized for 5 minutes.

Ms. MCSALLY. Thank you, Mr. Chairman. Thanks, all of you, for your testimony.

I think you have talked about it at some level, but some of the conversations I have had with some of the leadership in the services is about it not being a win-lose and a finite pie when we are looking at this as a nation.

We have requirements for our airlines, and a good, strong, growing economy and airline industry is good. We have requirements for our military. And if we are looking at this as a finite pie and win-lose, in the end, we are not going to be able to compete, prob- ably, with quality of life and, you know, resources, and especially at a time where pilots are not flying and, because of sequestration, they are doing more "queep" and all the stuff that drives you crazy, right, and impact on the family.

So what are you all thinking innovatively about turning this into a win-win, to partner with the airlines for individuals to be able to fly in the military and maybe have seasons of flying with the airlines and then come back for a 3-year tour later on and then go back to the airlines, so that we are partnering together and we are all winning as opposed to competing with each other?

General GROSSO. So, ma'am, our chief is meeting with the senior executives in the airline industry, and we are looking at just that. And based on the authorities that Congress has already given us with the Career Intermission Program, we are going to see if we can get, to your point, a win-win and get some predictability for the airmen, who may want to start their line number early, and get predictability for the Air Force and how can we get a better win-win.

And we are also starting to look at can we allow aviators to fly part-time on their own.

So I think those are just two ideas, and there are, I think, many more ways to think about this, for the Nation to get a win-win between the military and the private sector.

Ms. MCSALLY. Yeah, I totally agree. And when you think about the bonus and people at that 12-year point, you know, taking the bonus, in the past, maybe you get somebody inching towards the 13, 14, with the old retirement system, even if they didn't necessarily want to stay, they would start to make a decision like, "Well, I might as well just suck it up and get to 20 now." I mean, not everyone is like me, thinking about getting out at 18, the last time that I previously did. Most normal people, I think, as they get closer to 20.

Are you concerned about the blended retirement system and that not providing a hook, you know, to bridge them from, say, 13, 14 to 20 now, that they have the option to leave? Is that, do you think, going to be a factor?

General GROSSO. Well, we are concerned because we really don't know. We do a lot of force modeling, and we know how the old retirement system pulls people. So you are exactly right. But we do have that continuation pay in the new retirement system, and the intent of that is to get people to 20. So we are going to have to be very agile at executing that.

Ms. MCSALLY. Any other services?

Admiral BURKE. I would just add, we thank you for the help in the fiscal year 2017 NDAA that gave us the flexibility of the timing on that continuation period. That was very important to us, because we see that as a component, with existing retention tools that we have. Because, you know, we are going to probably have to modulate those other retention tools, along with that continuation pay, to influence retention behavior. So, together, we think we will be able to influence the behavior that we need to get them to 20 and beyond.

Ms. MCSALLY. Great. Thanks.

I think, you know, the career intermission is a great first step in a direction of—I just think, in general, the next generation, they want to be able to move in and out of the workforce, go get dif-ferent experiences. I think we need to open up that revolving door. And when you think about the millions of dollars it takes to bring somebody to become a 10-year pilot, for example—how long does it take to replace a 10-year pilot, right? It is a joke, right? Ten years—many of them got out and didn't go to the airlines. Maybe they, you know, went to start a business of their own or they tried some other—grass is always greener, and now they are realizing they miss the camaraderie, they miss the mission.

So I would really urge you to look—and it is challenging to try and find these people—where are the experienced pilots that have left? Maybe they are 2, 3, 5, 8 years out. It doesn't matter. I mean, retraining them, with the experience they have had, and bringing them back even for one assignment is worth the investment if you can find them.

Are you doing any initiatives to go find those that are not in the airlines but, you know, working in many different sectors of the economy?

General BRILAKIS. We have a Return to Active Duty Program. It has to be a short MOS. We are looking for the talent. I am not quite sure we ever looked at anybody being away for 6 or 8 years. Still have a PFT [physical fitness test] to get past. But we are open to those opportunities.

Ms. MCSALLY. Yeah, I just think it is that kind of, sort of, innovation that we have to be thinking of in order to not say, "Oh, we have to produce some more pilots," and just start at the beginning of, you know, the line again.

General BRILAKIS. Yes, ma'am. We have had conversations with industry as well, similar to what General Grosso discussed. And we are taking a look at the CIP [Career Intermission Program] and how we could fit that into a model that works for us.

Admiral BURKE. One of the items that we are working on under Sailor 2025 is more permeability between the Active and Reserve Components in the Navy. We are nowhere near as permeable as the Army and Air Force are and would like to get more.

But, recently, we brought a number of Reserve Component airline pilots now, but they were former naval aviators, in to help us stand up our remote-pilot Triton project down in Jacksonville. And, you know, they wanted to stay, so we were able to help them out. So, after having gone to the airline industry, they wanted to come back. So there is a little bit of that dynamic as well.

Ms. MCSALLY. Great. Thanks. I am out of time. I appreciate it.

Mr. COFFMAN. Thank you, Ms. McSally.

Vice Admiral Burke, going back to this retention bonus structure, can you brief the subcommittee in terms of what you are looking at right now in terms of a bonus retention structure?

Admiral BURKE. Yes, sir. Our current structure right now, we have two main points of concern. So our department head area is the most critical, and that applies for lieutenant commanders. And we pay by type/model/series or community, the type that they are flying. Our most critical needs right now are electronic attack aircraft, strike fighters, and then helicopter mine countermeasures.

And those folks are getting the top rates, and we are paying them at—current rate is $25,000 per year. And then, depending on type/model/series, others are less. And they are eligible for that after they finish their initial obligation, which is 8 years after winging. So typical winging occurs at about the 3——

Mr. COFFMAN. Define "winging."

Admiral BURKE. Yeah, at 3 years. You get your aviator wings at about the 3-year point after you finish flight school.

Mr. COFFMAN. Okay.

Admiral BURKE. So it is probably somewhere between 10 and 11 years of commissioned service is when your Active Duty service obligation is over.

So they become eligible for this bonus. And this bonus now obligates them for 5 years, which takes them through a department head tour and all the way through. If for some reason they don't select for O–4, they don't make it through their department head tour, we recoup.

Mr. COFFMAN. Oh.

Admiral BURKE. So, you know, they don't get paid for that which they do not serve.

So there is that aspect of it, and then we vary the rates. We put some economic factors in there. We have some economic modeling that we base the rates on. It is not extremely sophisticated. It is the best that we have available to us. We are working to get much more predictive analytics behind it and make it more sophisticated as we go forward.

And then our second critical zone is the post command level. So the first command opportunity is at the O–5 for commander level in the Navy, and then we ask them to obligate to the post-com- mand level. There are numerous post-command jobs on aircraft car- riers, such as, you know, the operations officers, the air bosses, things like that, that run critical operations on aircraft carriers. And we need them to obligate to stick around a little bit longer. And we structure that bonus to keep them at least through the window where they would make O–6, the theory being that, once they make O–6, they will stick around a little bit longer. So that is a 2-year bonus at $18,000 per year.

And both of those have had some positive effect. We are not getting exactly the response we want, so we are going to tweak both of those this year, both in terms of the bands and the numbers a little bit. But we don't expect to make full use of the legislative authority that you have given us, but we are going to move them both a little bit up in each direction.

One of the ideas that we are looking at here is something that we did in the surface warfare community last year. We tied merit to the bonuses, as well as need, and early-look screeners for the next milestone. So, in the case of aviators, if you screen early for department head, that is based on a look at your professional performance. The idea would be perhaps they are eligible for the bonus earlier and could get extra payments for it, thereby you are securing a contract with the best talent sooner.

Mr. COFFMAN. Okay.

Admiral BURKE. So we are looking at structuring something along those lines.

But, right now, we are paying for those two specific windows at a fraction of the available authority you have given us.

Mr. COFFMAN. Okay. Major General Peterson, United States Army, what is your approach in terms of retention bonuses going forward?

General PETERSON. Sir, we are looking at two specific targeted windows at the outset. First is at the cessation of their obligation for flight school, which is the 6-year mark. That will be the first hook for a multiyear commitment subsequent to that. And then at the retirement window, to retain that talent subsequently.

It is too early for us to tell the impacts of the blended retirement and the opportunities that may pull that window left to that 15-year mark. But we are looking for those leading indicators.

And then, last, we are exploring warrant officer aviation incentives, not tied to merit, but tied to actual, objective qualifications for advanced qualifications and skills, sir.

Mr. COFFMAN. Fair enough.

Let me just say one thing to all the services, in that I believe that this situation is temporary, this national shortage of pilots. And my concern is what always seems to happen in government is that there is a response to it and somehow there is a feeling that, once that response is baked in, that it is permanent.

And I just want to stress that this is really a temporary solution to a temporary problem. And I fully expect that we will come up—that you will come up with dynamic measures that, as this problem recedes, that these retention bonuses recede.

Ms. Speier.

Ms. SPEIER. Thank you, Mr. Chairman.

You know, I would also like to point out that I have a friend who did over 30 years at United Airlines as a captain, and, you know, pilots talk. And the United Airlines retirement system went belly up, and instead of getting $150,000 a year in retirement benefits per year, it was reduced to something like $60,000. So that is something to remember, too, in terms of the solid nature of the retirement system that exists in the U.S. Government.

So a couple of quick questions, and I won't belabor any of this.

General Grosso, there was a time in the not-so-distant past when the Air Force was giving the same bonus out to all pilots regardless of whether there was a particular need in a particular specialty so that, you know, a tanker pilot was getting the same bonus as a fighter pilot.

Have you changed that now so that it reflects more in terms of what your need is?

General GROSSO. Yes, ma'am, we have. And I can give you great detail when you have time.

Ms. SPEIER. Okay. I was kind of alarmed when I heard, in answer to one of my colleagues' questions about the continuing resolution, that we would conceivably be in a position where we offered a bonus to an aviator and then, because we are doing a CR instead of an appropriation, that we end up reneging on that bonus. Is that what happens?

General BRILAKIS. The challenge in the CR, if it wasn't authorized in the previous year, we are not authorized to pay it. And so, if we had planned to a pay a bonus in the fiscal year 2018 timeframe that we weren't paying—and, remember, we are going to be doing a bonus for the first time in 6 years, so it is not in our 2017 budget. It wasn't in our 2016 budget, and so it won't be available to us in this 2017 year budget. And the flexibility, we will have to reprogram—have to go for a specific reprogramming action to free up the dollars to be able to do that.

Ms. SPEIER. But we now have a contract with this aviator to give him this bonus, and we are reneging on it? Or you are saying we are reprogramming dollars so you are able to pay that bonus?

General BRILAKIS. It is about reprogramming money.

Ms. SPEIER. Got it. Okay. I think it is really important not to renege on these bonuses. I think that would be a disaster in the making.

I think it was you, General Brilakis, who was talking about parts, was it not? Or was it you, Admiral Burke?

General BRILAKIS. I did, ma'am. I think we both——

Ms. SPEIER. Okay. So we have been focused on the pilots, but, as you pointed out, if you don't have the parts to fix the planes, the pilot can't fly. And what are we doing about the mechanics? Is there a shortage of mechanics that we should be addressing as well? Could you just——

General BRILAKIS. So, for our part, on the enlisted maintainer side, our challenge is not necessarily the number, but it is also experience. Your aviation maintenance marine gets his basic training in his field, but on top of that there are additional certifications. Because aircrafters are so critical, and the fact is, every time you go up, we want you to come down in the same way, they have certifications that are required. Those certifications take time, upwards of a year or multiple years to receive all the different certifications so you can sign off on the maintenance.

Our challenge has been, in the drawdown, the availability of those marines with those experiences, et cetera. So, on the enlisted side, while we do pay retention bonuses to manage the numbers, we are also pursuing in the beginning of this next retention year what we call an op-4 kicker, an additional payment for marines who are willing to reenlist and then go, in that 4-year reenlistment, 24 months in the squadron, retaining those capabilities.

Because, more often than not, a marine who reenlists has a location option. He may want to go to recruiting duty or at the drill field, because our marines serve across the Marine Corps. This bonus is going to take that experience, hard-won experience, at the senior sergeant staff NCO level, retain it in the squadron in certain numbers, so they can train the next generation in those certification requirements. That is new for us.

Ms. SPEIER. Anyone else have any comments about mechanics?

Admiral BURKE. We are in good shape, mechanics.

Ms. SPEIER. Okay.

Admiral BURKE. We just——

Ms. SPEIER. All right.

General GROSSO. Ma'am, we are short mechanics. Based on decisions made in the 2014 President's budget, we are ramping up accessions and having no trouble bringing new airmen in. But, obviously, there will be an experience gap. We expect to be balanced in fiscal year 2019.

General PETERSON. We are reasonably strong with respect to our mechanics. However, we do have experience challenges that have been brought on by force management levels in recent years where mechanics have not deployed with their units and they have been replaced by contractors. We are overcoming that now, but we will not regain that years of experience.

Ms. SPEIER. Mr. Chairman, I want to ask this last question, but I do want everyone to think about it.

We are not using aviators in the same way, in all likelihood, that we have used them in past wars. And with the advent of drones, I think we all have to think about the makeup of our forces in terms of the technological advances that have taken place and how we are going to engage in subsequent actions around the world.

And, with that, I yield back.

Mr. COFFMAN. Thank you, Ranking Member Speier.

Just a very quick point, Major General Peterson. That entire issue with force management levels and leaving maintenance personnel behind so that we don't reach some artificial cap in Afghanistan and use private contractors in their stead was a horrible decision, in my view. And it is something that this subcommittee needs to revisit and make sure that it never occurs again.

I wish to thank the witnesses for their testimony this afternoon. This has been very informative.

There being no further business, the subcommittee stands adjourned.

[Whereupon, at 3:21 p.m., the subcommittee was adjourned.]

A P P E N D I X

March 29, 2017

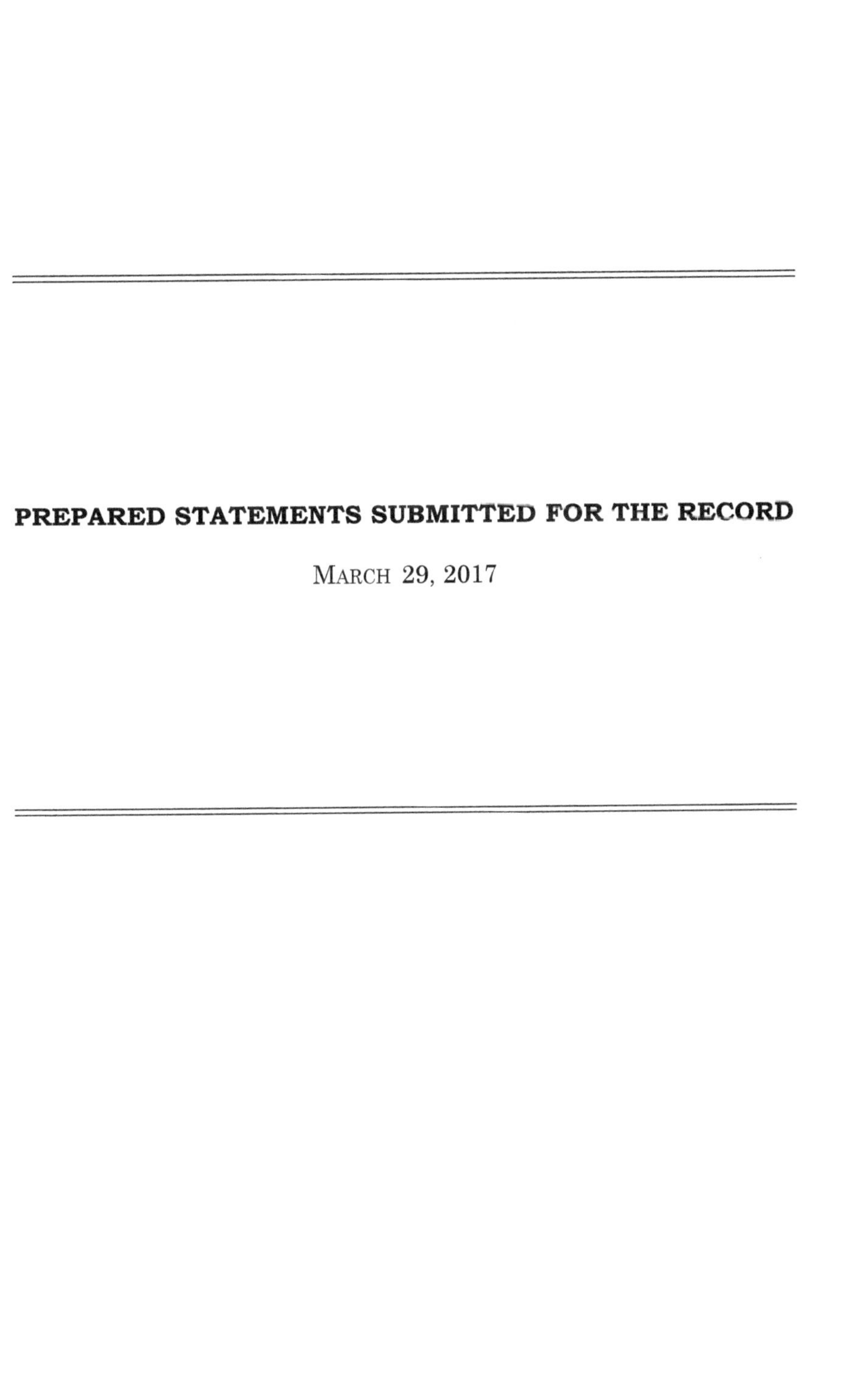

PREPARED STATEMENTS SUBMITTED FOR THE RECORD

March 29, 2017

Opening Remarks – Chairman Coffman
Military Personnel Subcommittee Hearing
Military Pilot Shortage
March 29, 2017

I want to welcome everyone to the Military Personnel Subcommittee hearing on the shortage of pilots in the military services. Today we will hear from the services on their progress toward increasing the retention of military pilots, both officers and warrant officers. We know that pilot demand is increasing in the commercial sector and the demand to hire qualified military pilots is higher than the available pool of candidates. This demand has led to a shortage of pilots across the Services with the problem being particularly acute in the Air Force, with the deficit at this point of over 1,000 total pilots. This trend cannot continue and we are here today to hear from the Armed Services on their plans to stem the exit of pilots from the military. We know we cannot buy our way out of this problem since the military cannot compete with the potential salaries—and in some cases the lifestyle—of the commercial airlines. So we must make sure the Services are using all the levers in their control—from an increase in bonuses to changes in the assignment system to changes in promotions—to incentivize these pilots to remain in service.

The Military Personnel Subcommittee will take every opportunity to thoroughly review and discuss the way forward to stop the outflow of military pilots.

I look forward to hearing from the witnesses to understand the scope of the pilot retention problem and to assess the proposed resolutions for the Services in increasing retention.

Before I introduce our panel, let me offer Ranking Member Speier an opportunity to make any opening remarks.

STATEMENT

OF

LIEUTENANT GENERAL MARK A. BRILAKIS

DEPUTY COMMANDANT FOR MANPOWER & RESERVE AFFAIRS

UNITED STATES MARINE CORPS

BEFORE THE

SUBCOMMITTEE ON PERSONNEL

OF THE

HOUSE ARMED SERVICES COMMITTEE

CONCERNING

AVIATOR MANPOWER

ON

29 MARCH 2017

INTRODUCTION

Chairman Coffman, Ranking Member Speier, and distinguished Members of the Subcommittee, it is my privilege to appear before you today to provide an overview on Marine Corps aviator inventory.

Since the first Marine aviator flew in 1912, our aviators, like all Marines, have answered our Nation's call, faithfully serving the American people and maintaining a first class standard of military excellence. Your Marine Corps is, and will continue to be, our Nation's expeditionary force in readiness. We will be ready to rapidly respond to crises around the globe, to ensure the continued security of the American people, and to protect the interests that underpin our Nation. Marines will be *always faithful* to the trust which the American people have vested in them. Everything we do in the Marine Corps must contribute to their combat readiness and combat effectiveness.

AVIATION RETENTION

Our aviation Marines, those that operate the aircraft and the officers and enlisted Marines who are responsible for their maintenance, are a critical component of how the Marine Corps trains and fights. We vigorously track the accession and retention of all of our Marine occupational fields, and doing so for the aviation field is particularly important due to the time and expense required to train the majority of the Marines that make up this field. Our analysis shows that the Marine Corps is currently not experiencing a retention challenge for our aviators or enlisted maintenance Marines. While there are imbalances in grade and occupational fields, current aggregate inventory levels are at 100% of overall requirement. Our aviators generally have a higher retention rate than our ground Marine officers. This has been true for the past 30 years and is still true today. All of our officer occupational fields, aviation and ground, experienced an intentional increase in attrition rates during the drawdown period from 2012 to 2015 as we encouraged specific grades to separate or retire from the service. During the drawdown period, we also reduced the size of accession cohorts for the same reason. Now that our drawdown has concluded, and we are implementing a modest end strength increase, attrition is trending back down to our lower rates associated with stabilized end strength.

In regard to future commercial airline hiring, we note that the majority of Marine Corps aviators are from rotary wing and tilt-rotor communities. These aviation communities have historically been in less demand than the pilots of jet and larger multi-engine aircraft. Since the Marine Corps inventory is directly managed to meet structural grade/MOS requirements, a certain level of attrition is healthy, and in fact, required to be able to maintain our grade/MOS designs. At this time, our current and forecast aviator attrition rates do not exceed this healthy level and we have no data indicating that there is any specific draw for Marine aviators to depart the service in numbers greater than forecast. However, we will continue to closely monitor the retention trends of our aviators and take action should we begin to see a change in this arena.

TRAINING CHALLENGE

Training for our aviation community is both long and expensive. It begins with ground-based instruction in aerodynamics and instrumentation, and progressing first to primary flight training in basic aircraft and then to advanced instrument flight and military formations in advanced tactical aircraft. Training continues in the operating forces as winged aviators continue to progress in more advanced tactical maneuvers. Training schedules are complex and must be coordinated as training squadrons compete for limited training ranges and airfield hours.

Currently, our initial training pipelines are experiencing challenges that are impacting aviation platforms in the operating force, primarily at the Company Grade level. Due to readiness issues with training aircraft, e.g. parts supply issues, it is taking longer to train our pilots. As a result, there is currently a number of aviators in the training pipeline who normally would already be in the fleet squadrons. Fortunately, higher ranking aviators, Majors and above, are currently making up for this shortfall. Still, we are exploring a targeted monetary bonus for Captains who have completed their initial undergraduate pilot obligation and some Majors in specific challenged inventories in order to encourage even higher retention. The specific and targeted nature of these potential bonuses will provide us the ability to increase and expand these incentives should we begin to see problems arise in our aviator retention rate.

AVIATION READINESS

Another challenge impacting our aviation community, and the Marine Corps overall, is degraded aviation readiness. Since the conclusion of the combat operations in Iraq and Afghanistan, degraded aviation readiness is making it difficult to replace the advanced instructor and combat qualifications many of these aviators currently hold. Addressing readiness is one of our highest priorities. Independent Readiness Reviews with each of our aviation platforms are providing external assessments from independent experts to reveal current readiness issues for targeted solutions. The increased funding we've received for readiness, reliability, consumables, and parts is beginning to positively impact readiness. Additionally, we continue to modernize and transition into our new airframes, like the MV-22, AH-1Z and the F-35. Adequate manning will continue to be critical as we outfit with new aircraft while maintaining our operational tempo and strive to improve readiness. A continued commitment to investing in the modernization of our legacy aircraft is paramount to our plans to return to an optimal state of readiness and combat any potential retention problems that may otherwise be on the horizon.

CONCLUSION

The bottom line is that the Marine Corps does not currently have a shortage of aviators, as measured against our aggregate structural requirement, however we are experiencing a shortage of trained aviators, particularly in specific platforms, due to training and readiness issues with our aircraft. These aviators are critical to our ability to fulfill continued and increasing operational commitments, high operational tempo, and challenging deployment-to-dwell ratios. Overall, training time and full-mission ready aircraft, as well as pay, are all important factors in an aviator's and maintainer's decision to stay or depart the service. We take seriously our responsibility to train and retain the best aviators and maintainers for our Corps. We will continue our rigorous tracking of retention in the aviation field so that your Corps remains the most ready when the Nation is least ready.

The Marines of our Corps represent the American people who have stepped forward and sworn to defend and protect our Nation. Our individual Marines are our most precious asset. They are proud of what they do. They are proud of the "Eagle, Globe, and Anchor" and what it represents to our Nation. With your support, a vibrant Marine Corps will continue to meet our Nation's call.

Thank you for the opportunity to present this testimony.

Lieutenant General Mark A. Brilakis
Deputy Commandant for Manpower and Reserve Affairs

Lieutenant General Mark Andrew Brilakis is currently assigned as the Deputy Commandant for Manpower and Reserve Affairs.

He graduated from Franklin and Marshall College, Lancaster, Pennsylvania, and was commissioned through the Platoon Leaders Class in May 1981.

Assignments in the Operating Forces include: Battery Officer, 1st Battalion, 10th Marines; Battery Commander, Battalion FDO, and S-3, 5th Battalion, 10th Marines; Naval Gunfire Control Officer and Assistant Supporting Arms Coordinator, Amphibious Group Two; Future Operations and MAGTF Planner, G-3, II MEF; Executive Officer, 10th Marine Regiment; Commanding Officer 1st Battalion, 10th Marines; Commanding General, 3d Marine Expeditionary Brigade, Deputy Commanding General, III Marine Expeditionary Force, and Commanding General, 3d Marine Division.

Assignments in the Supporting Establishment include: Company Officer and Commanding Officer, Company A, and Course Developer, MCI Company, Marine Barracks, Washington DC; Commanding Officer, Weapons Training Battalion, Training Command; and the Commanding General, Marine Corps Recruiting Command.

Headquarters and Staff assignments include: Status of Forces Officer, Plans, Policies, and Operations Department, HQMC; Head, Program Development Branch, Programs and Resources Department, HQMC; Director, European Liaison Office, Headquarters, U.S. European Command, Deputy J-3, United States European Command, and Assistant Deputy Commandant (Programs), Programs & Resources Department, HQMC.

Military Education: Amphibious Warfare School; Command and Staff College; School of Advanced Warfighting; and CMC Fellow, Center for Strategic and International Studies. Masters in Military Studies, Marine Corps University.

**NOT FOR PUBLICATION UNTIL
RELEASED BY THE HOUSE
ARMED SERVICES COMMITTEE**

STATEMENT OF

VICE ADMIRAL ROBERT P. BURKE, U.S. NAVY

CHIEF OF NAVAL PERSONNEL

AND

DEPUTY CHIEF OF NAVAL OPERATIONS

(MANPOWER, PERSONNEL, TRAINING and EDUCATION)

BEFORE THE

SUBCOMMITTEE ON MILITARY PERSONNEL

OF THE

HOUSE ARMED SERVICES COMMITTEE

ON

PILOT SHORTAGES

MARCH 29, 2017

**NOT FOR PUBLICATION UNTIL
RELEASED BY THE HOUSE
ARMED SERVICES COMMITTEE**

INTRODUCTION

Chairman Coffman, Ranking Member Speier, distinguished Members of the Subcommittee, thank you for this opportunity to discuss the status of Navy Aviation retention.

I am here to outline the current risks and projected manning challenges facing Navy aviation and what we must do to ensure we sustain combat readiness. The thriving civilian market offers strong employment alternatives to aviation officers, and we are keeping a close eye on retention. High-tempo operational environments combined with decreased readiness have added additional pressures on these highly skilled aviators and lead to decreasing retention rates. We must address current and future shortfalls through continued judicious application of targeted incentives and non-monetary retention tools, aimed at retaining required personnel and sustaining required readiness levels. Aviators are keenly watching the many quality of life and service initiatives Navy leadership is undertaking, while monitoring increasing opportunities and associated incentives available in the recovering civilian aviation market.

AVIATOR RETENTION VERSUS REQUIREMENTS

Our ability to attract and retain the very best young men and women our nation has to offer is central to maintaining aviation personnel readiness. A number of factors have made this challenge increasingly difficult and complex, including an improving economy with low unemployment. Navy aviator retention through department head assignment, nominally the 10-12 year career point, has fallen below the three, five, and ten year average continuation rates, a trend that is expected to continue for the foreseeable future. While mid-level officer retention represents our greatest challenge, resignations have also increased among junior and senior aviators due, in part, to intense competition from private industry. Post-command commander (O-5) losses have steadily increased since 2009, further diminishing essential talent and experience. Navy is also experiencing a smaller pool of officers entering the window for department head assignment, which drives retention rate requirements above historic averages to meet operational requirements. Retention among some communities must increase significantly over the next several years to maintain operational squadron department head requirements.

It is absolutely vital that we retain mid-level and senior aviators, capitalizing on their experience, leadership, and the multi-million dollar investment they represent to ensure maximum combat readiness and ability to execute the National Military Strategy.

WHY ARE AVIATORS LEAVING?

Aviators are leaving the Navy for two primary reasons: The first reason is increasing opportunity and pay in the Airlines. The second reason is dissatisfaction with the Navy due to readiness challenges that have limited aircraft availability and resulted in reduced flying hours and associated tactical qualifications, and in some cases, have impacted career progression. According to feedback from the latest Aviation Department Head Decliner Survey, aviators are dissatisfied with other quality of service issues to include operational tempo, excessive administrative burdens, and low incentive pay when compared to opportunities outside the Navy, as well as quality of life issues for their families, including late PCS orders, reduced health care/child care availability, and limited housing options, especially in non-fleet concentration areas.

The airline industry is emerging from a decade of consolidation and restructuring and is positioned for greater stability in the foreseeable future, which, when coupled with mandatory retirement age, working hours, and global hiring can be expected to exert a significant pull on military pilots as reorganized airlines enhance their compensation offerings. Independent industry analysts have confirmed the forecasted hiring of 50,000 airline pilots over the next 10 years, representing an approximate 400 percent increase, or 2,000-3,000 pilot increase per year, and the hiring has begun. Additionally, the total airline career income and benefit packages are lucrative in light of their first-year pay scales. As the economy continues to improve and airlines offer increased pay, we must have the ability to retain needed aviator inventory to maintain mission readiness.

In 2007, the law governing the age at which commercial pilots must retire changed from 60 to 65. December 2012 marked the fifth anniversary of the increased retirement age and the airlines are beginning to see the results of the mandatory retirements. Approximately 30,000 pilots will retire from global and major airlines in the next ten years.

Naval aviators are a prime target of the industry. In July 2013, the Federal Aviation Administration (FAA) increased the minimum number of flight hours required to be eligible for employment to fly a commercial aircraft from 250 to 1,500. Navy pilots typically reach 1,500 hours as lieutenants while under their initial minimum service obligations. Industry analysts expect that global and major airlines will need to aggressively recruit pilots with military backgrounds to make up commercial pilot shortfall projections. Discussions about the opportunity for quicker upgrades to airline captain (more rapid pay increases) as the hiring pace surges among commercial airlines are cause for concern within the Naval Aviation Enterprise as well as for the aviation communities of other services.

Navy's largest internal retention factors include readiness. Retention impacts readiness and readiness impacts retention. We must view these issues in tandem and understand that struggles to maintain the proper numbers and skillsets of aviators, manifests in readiness risk. In turn, readiness issues affect quality of service and quality of life, influencing retention behavior. As Sailors prepare to ensure our next aircraft squadrons deploy with all that they need, the strain is significant. Aviation depots struggle to get our airplanes through maintenance periods on time. In turn, these delays directly impact the time Sailors have to train and hone their skills prior to deployment. These challenges are further exacerbated by low stocks of critical parts and an aging shore infrastructure. While our first team on deployment is ready, our bench – the depth of our forces at home – is thin.

There are three main drivers of our readiness problems: 1) persistent, high operational demand for naval forces, 2) funding constraints, and 3) continued uncertainty about when those budgets will be approved.

- The operational demand for our Navy continues to be high, while the fleet has gotten smaller. Between 2001 and 2015, Navy was able to keep an average of 100 ships at sea each day, despite a 14 percent decrease in the size of the battle force. The fleet is smaller today than it has been in the last 99 years. Maintaining current deployment levels has taken a significant toll on Sailors and their families, as well as on our equipment.

- The second factor degrading Navy readiness is the result of several years of constrained funding levels for our major readiness accounts, largely due to fiscal pressures imposed by the Budget Control Act of 2011.

- The third primary driver of reduced readiness is the inefficiency imposed by the uncertainty around when, and if, budgets will actually be approved. The inability to adjust funding levels as planned, or to commit to longer-term contracts, creates additional work while driving up costs. This results in even less capability for any given dollar we invest, and represents yet another tax on our readiness. We are underfunded and spending more time to maintain a less ready Navy.

Attempts to address maintenance and training backlogs resulting from high operational tempo have been further exacerbated by budget caps included in the Budget Control Act and fiscal uncertainty. Our attempts to restore stability and predictability to deployment cycles have been challenged both by constrained funding levels and by high operational demands. Although we remain committed to return to a seven month deployment cycle as the norm, the need to support the fight against ISIS compelled our extending deployments in 2016 up to eight and a half months, in some cases. This collective pace of operations has increased wear-and-tear on aircraft and crews and has added to the downward decline in readiness, lower retention, and decreasing available time for maintenance and modernization. Deferred maintenance has led to equipment failures, and to larger-than-projected scope of work for aviation depots. This has forced us to remove aircraft from service for extended periods, thus increasing the utilization of the rest of the fleet and forcing them to use airframes at higher-than-projected rates, which further increases maintenance workload and reduces depot output.

Reversing this vicious cycle and restoring short-term readiness of the fleet will require sufficient and consistent funding. This funding would allow our pilots to fly the hours they need to remain proficient, recapitalize our expended aircraft and ensure that we can conduct required maintenance on those airframes we need to retain. It would also enable Navy to restore stocks of necessary parts, get more aircraft ready to fly and better prepare them to remain deployed as required.

Years of sustained deployments and constrained and uncertain funding have resulted in having to retain aircraft beyond their design life, and exacerbate the readiness debt, which will take years to alleviate. If the slow pace of readiness recovery and declining retention continue the result will be poorly trained operators at sea, and a force improperly trained and equipped to sustain itself. This also jeopardizes the lives of our Sailors. Absent sufficient funding for readiness, retention, modernization and recapitalization of force structure, Navy cannot return to full health, where we can continue to meet our mission on a sustainable basis. As we strive to improve efficiency in internal business practices, those efforts are being actively undermined by the absence of regular and timely budgets. Although we face many readiness challenges, we remain committed to maintaining the finest naval aviation force in the world. That commitment will require constant vigilance and a dedication to retention and readiness recovery, in full partnership with the Congress.

WHAT ARE WE DOING ABOUT IT?

The commercial airline industry is expected to hire at an increased level for an extended duration, providing a lucrative alternative for highly sought after Navy aviators with requisite knowledge and experience. Navy cannot compete dollar for dollar with private industry, particularly America's airlines. Nonetheless, enhanced military compensation will be a fundamental factor in any long-range solution to ensure adequate retention in undermanned, highly skilled, warfare specialties.

The primary monetary tools supporting aviator retention are Aviation Career Incentive Pay (ACIP) and Aviation Continuation Pay (ACP), recently changed to Aviation Incentive Pay (AvIP) and Aviation Bonus (AvB) respectively. Congress' recent enactment of an increase in the statutory cap for AvB was well-received and appreciated by aviators. The National Defense Authorization Act (NDAA) for Fiscal Year 2017 increased the AvB maximum annual amount payable from $25,000 to $35,000 per year, and the AvIP from $850 to $1,000 per month. Navy is working options for a judicious approach to utilizing these increases in a responsible and cost-effective manner.

Navy offers two aviation retention bonuses targeting aviators at critical career decision points: Aviation Department Head Retention Bonus (ADHRB) offered to lieutenants (O3) and lieutenant commanders (O4), and Aviation Command Retention Bonus (ACRB) offered to commanders (O5s). Historically, these targeted bonuses have proven effective and cost-efficient in attacking retention problems in specific communities, jobs, and experience levels, in a cost-effective way so as to attract and retain high-quality personnel to meet fleet requirements.

Effective implementation of these programs is critical to our effort to influence retention behavior. As aviators accessed during fiscal years 2005-12 near completion of their active duty service obligation, the challenge to retain high-quality aviators is increasing. We will continue to review the adequacy of compensation and the effectiveness of our programs to initiate efficient solutions.

It is imperative that we maintain adequate numbers of quality career force aviators to fill operational billets, not only at the department head level, but also for second sea, command and post-command tours. The ACRB is designed to retain post-command commanders (O5) into the grade of captain (O6). For FY2010, the bonus amount was reduced from $45,000 to $36,000, and in FY2012 it was canceled. Perhaps not coincidently, the number of post-command commanders leaving the Navy has steadily increased since 2009. In an effort to reverse this trend, a restructured version of the program was reinstated for FY2015 at $36,000 but the structure of the program has not yet sufficiently influenced retention behavior, and we continue to lose aviators with vital experience and leadership.

Not surprisingly, the "take rate" of retention bonuses has proven to be an accurate indicator of aviator retention behavior. While some individual type/model/series and designators have achieved their individual department head bonus contract goals, the Navy has not achieved the overall department head bonus contract goal since 2013. To address the decline in aviator retention as these bonuses lose their effectiveness, Navy is examining a plan to leverage the recently increased cap to target specific communities with retention issues that are exposing operational manning requirements to increased levels of risk.

Signed bonus contracts are used as a proxy for indications of retention to ensure the department head requirements are met. While some communities are meeting their requirements, other communities have struggled. Fleet requirements have been met through distribution mitigation methods to offset shortfalls, such as transitioning pilots from one community to another. Navy is considering increased bonus amounts for Strike Fighters (VFA), Electronic Attack (VAQ), and Helicopter Mine Countermeasure (HM) aviators. Of immediate concern is VFA and VAQ pilot manning.

For example, we are currently experiencing a chronic shortfall among VAQ pilots, for which we have not retained sufficient numbers of O-4s to meet fleet department head requirements since May 2011. For active duty year groups 2004-2006, we have attained less than half of required VAQ pilot department heads (16 of 34). If all four of the remaining VAQ pilots in year groups 2005 and 2006 sign bonus contracts, the best possible outcome is 20 retained of 34 required. Consequently, we have been forced to transition some junior Strike Fighter (VFA) pilots into the VAQ community, upon selection to department head, to ensure that deploying VAQ squadrons were fully manned with O-4 pilots. This, however, is only a temporary solution since VFA has also begun to experience declining retention, falling short of its pilot manpower requirement.

Similar to VAQ, for the active duty year groups 2004 to 2006, we only have signed contracts for three-quarters of our required VFA pilot department heads (116 of 149). While 52 remain eligible to sign bonus contracts, trend data indicates only a quarter of these will contract, yielding a predicted best possible outcome of thirteen additional pilots or 129 of the 149 required. This situation will become dire if retention trends in these communities continue their downward trajectory.

Navy's reserve support type/model/series needs are also reflective of these shortages, with smaller, but no less significant, retention issues for VAQ, HM, and Maritime Patrol (VP). Navy is also evaluating additional incentives for aviators with high demand subspecialties such as Weapons Tactics Instructors and Test Pilots.

In addition to bonuses, Navy continues to assess and pursue non-monetary incentives to improve retention across the force, as outlined in Sailor 2025, a dynamic set of approximately 45 initiatives designed to help us do just that. Built on a framework of three pillars - a modernized personnel system, ready relevant learning, and career readiness - Sailor 2025 is a roadmap designed to change our approach to personnel programs by providing our personnel with choice and flexibility. These initiatives target modernizing personnel management and training systems to find, recruit, train, and manage the careers of our talented people more effectively, thus improving the Navy's warfighting readiness.

SUMMARY

Aviator retention remains a high priority. Navy is deliberate in managing the aviation officer communities and judicious in executing the respective aviation incentive pay programs. We are closely monitoring declining aviation retention trends. Manning mitigation techniques, such as tour extensions and junior officer re-tours, have minimized gaps, but low inventory coupled with declining retention have pressurized the distribution system. We remain firmly committed to improving our personnel readiness posture while addressing concerns of our outstanding aviation officers. Although aviation continues to be attractive to young people eager for a rewarding career in service of our country, continued and future low retention of experienced combat-proven aviators is not in the best interest of the nation or the combat readiness of the Navy.

Navy remains concerned regarding issues that impact the quality of service and life for aviators and their family to include: lack of spare parts and equipment, lack of flying hours, deployment frequency, and minimum-notice permanent change of station moves. Aviation officer retention is dramatically impacted by the relative strength of our compensation and bonus packages over time, as compared with the lure of a strong economy offering excellent opportunities for educated professionals, and a perception of increased quality of life in the civilian sector. Unfortunately, any declines in retention mean those remaining have to work that much harder to meet the demand for forward deployed naval forces and, in turn, further impacts retention. It is imperative that we continue to focus on improving aviation retention and incentives during this time of high competition for talent.

We will continue to aggressively pursue resolution of aviator retention challenges through effective use of all available resources. A comprehensive and competitive compensation package comprised of targeted special and incentive pays and bonuses, combined with quality of life and quality of service efforts, are essential to this effort. We look forward to working with you as we collectively work to address the challenges we face, and appreciate your continued support for initiatives designed to achieve optimum personnel readiness, improved quality of service, and retain the best and brightest young men and women this nation has to offer.

5/27/2016- Present

Vice Admiral Robert P. Burke

Vice Adm. Robert Burke grew up in Portage, Michigan, and holds bachelor's and master's degrees in electrical engineering from Western Michigan University and the University of Central Florida.

Burke's operational assignments include service aboard both attack and ballistic missile submarines, including USS Von Steuben (SSBN 632), USS Maryland (SSBN 738) and USS Bremerton (SSN 698). He commanded USS Hampton (SSN 767) in Norfolk, Virginia, and was commodore of Submarine Development Squadron (DEVRON) 12 in Groton, Connecticut. Burke was recognized by the United States Submarine League with the Jack Darby Award for Leadership in 2004 and the Vice Admiral James Bond Stockdale Award for Inspirational Leadership in 2005.

His staff assignments include tours as an instructor and director for the Electrical Engineering Division at Naval Nuclear Power School, junior board member on the Pacific Fleet Nuclear Propulsion Examining Board, submarine officer community manager/nuclear officer program manager; senior Tactical Readiness Evaluation Team member at Commander, Submarine Force, U.S. Atlantic Fleet; the deputy director for Operations, Strategy and Policy Directorate (J5) at United States Joint Forces Command; the division director, Submarine/Nuclear Power Distribution (PERS-42); and director, Joint and Fleet Operations, N3/N5, U.S. Fleet Forces Command.

As a flag officer, Burke has served as deputy commander,U.S.6th Fleet; director of operations (N3), U.S. Naval Forces Europe-Africa; commander, Submarine Group 8;and most recently as director, Military Personnel Plans and Policy (OPNAV N13).

He assumed duties as the Navy's 58th chief of naval personnel, May 27,2016.Serving concurrently as the deputy chief of naval operations (Manpower, Personnel, Training and Education) (N1), he is responsible for the planning and programming of all manpower, personnel, training and education resources for the U.S. Navy. He leads more than 26,000 employees engaged in the recruiting, personnel management, training and development of Navy personnel. His responsibilities include overseeing Navy Recruiting Command, Navy Personnel Command and Naval Education and Training Command.

His awards include the Defense Superior Service Medal, the Legion of Merit (five awards) and various campaign and unit awards.

Updated: 17 June 2016

DEPARTMENT OF THE AIR FORCE

PRESENTATION TO THE SUBCOMMITTEE ON PERSONNEL

COMMITTEE ON ARMED SERVICES

UNITED STATES HOUSE OF REPRESENTATIVES

SUBJECT: MILITARY PILOT SHORTAGE

STATEMENT OF:

      LIEUTENANT GENERAL GINA M. GROSSO
      DEPUTY CHIEF OF STAFF MANPOWER, PERSONNEL
      AND SERVICES UNITED STATES AIR FORCE

MARCH 29, 2017

NOT FOR PUBLICATION UNTIL RELEASED
BY THE COMMITTEE ON ARMED SERVICES
UNITED STATES HOUSE OF REPRESENTATIVES

INTRODUCTION

Your Air Force has been globally engaged for the last 26 years in combat operations. During that time, America's Air Force provided air dominance through ***global vigilance, global reach, and global power*** for our joint force. Make no mistake, your Air Force is always there.

However, being "always there" comes at a cost to equipment, infrastructure, and most importantly, our Airmen—and we are now at a decision point. Sustained global commitments and recent funding constraints have affected capacity and capability for a full-spectrum fight against a near-peer adversary. Compounding this issue, an upcoming surge of mandatory retirements for airline pilots and increasing market for global commerce is causing the civilian aviation industry to begin hiring at an aggressive rate. This confluence of circumstances has birthed a national aircrew crisis.

NATIONAL AIRCREW CRISIS

The national aircrew crisis is the result of multiple factors: high operational tempo over the last 26 years, a demand for our pilots from the commercial industry, and cultural issues that affect the quality of life and quality of service of our Airmen. At the end of FY 2016 the total force including active, reserve, and guard components was short 1,555 pilots across all mission areas (608 active, 653 guard, 294 reserve). Of this amount, the total force was short 1,211 fighter pilots (873 active, 272 guard, 66 reserve). Unfortunately, our greatest concern is the active fighter pilot shortage is projected exceed 1,000 by the end of FY 2017.

The nation requires Airmen to be "always there" to deliver air, space and cyber effects. These capabilities demand resources and time to train in order to ensure readiness. In the aircraft maintenance field, we were short approximately 3,400 aircraft maintainers at the close of 2016.

Because of this shortage, we cannot generate the sorties needed to fully train our aircrews. Though our end-strength has decreased 38% since 1991, we have experienced significant growth across several mission areas. The increased operational tempo levied on remaining personnel removes the time required to train for conflicts in different environments. A quarter-century at war has strained the force through reduced sortie rates and training availability. At current force structure levels the operational tempo and deployments that your Air Force maintains in order to support the joint force simply does not allow time for personnel to adequately train for future conflicts. More than an entire generation of airmen have prioritized operations over training. Our aircrews are not able to maintain full-spectrum readiness against all threats with these conditions.

Civilian aviation companies are actively recruiting the world-class experience of our rated Airmen. Air Force pilots are highly attractive because of their proficiency, diverse experience, and the standardization and quality of military aviation training. A 2016 RAND study, requested by FY16 NDAA and endorsed by OSD, modeled a potentially large growth in hiring in the airline industry over the next decade, which could require the Air Force to significantly increase retention efforts. RAND modeled major airline hiring levels between 3,200 – 3,800 pilots per year and an average 13 percent increase in airlines salaries. In reality, actual airline hiring and salary increases surpassed those predictions. According to Future and Active Pilot Advisors, major airlines hired more than 4,100 pilots last year and salaries increased by 17 percent. These annual hiring levels are expected to continue for the next 10-15 years (Table 1).

Table 1. Airline Hiring and Retirements

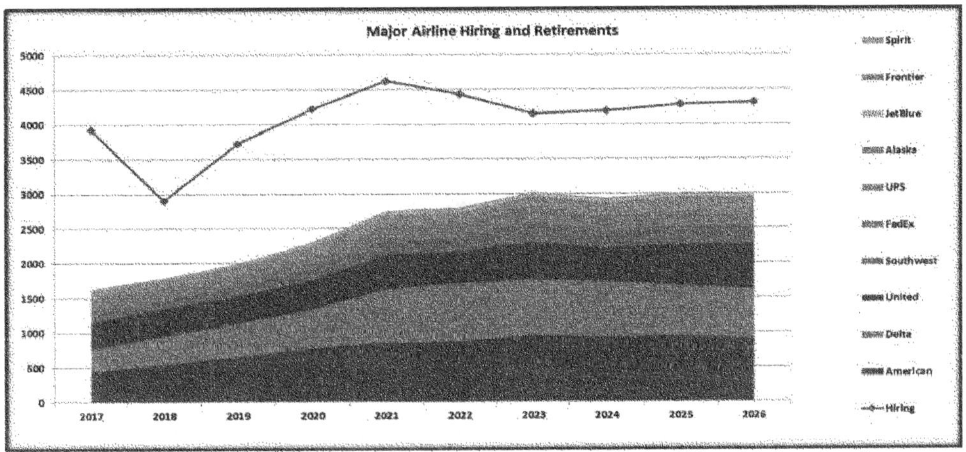

Sources: FAPA.aero/hiringhistory.asp (Future and Active Pilot Advisors) and
www.airlinepilotcentral.com/airlines/legacy/delta_air_lines

Table 2. 2015 Rated Exit Survey Results "Top 5 Influences to Leave"

Pilot Influences	Top 5
Additional Duties	37%
Maintaining work/life balance and meeting family commitments	31%
Availability of Civilian Jobs	24%
Home Station Tempo (length of duty day/work schedule)	22%
The potential to leave your family for a deployment	21%

Civilian job prospects are not the sole reason the Air Force is losing talent. A 2015 exit

survey revealed additional motives for separation, highlighting negative impacts to the quality of

life and quality of service of our aviators and their families (Table 2). Pilots are making choices

to leave the service on factors like additional duties (creating the daily flying schedule, vault security duties, ancillary training, and administrative support) maintaining a work-life balance, and the pace of work while at home from deployment. This combination of high operational tempo, civilian airline pilot demand, and cultural issues have created a perfect storm--one the Air Force is acting quickly to address. Your Air Force's action plan to mitigate these shortfalls is three-pronged: reduce requirements, increase production and increase retention.

MITIGATION EFFORTS – REDUCED REQUIREMENTS

The demand for rated pilot experience is insatiable. However, the Air Force no longer has available capacity to man historical requirements with pilots unless it is absolutely critical. The 2017 Rated Staff Allocation Plan reduced the total number of pilots assigned to institutional organizations by 13% when compared to 2016. These key staff positions, such as planners at Combatant Commands, Air Operations Centers, and Training units are currently manned at 23-26 percent for fighter pilot specific positions and 79-84 percent in all other rated positions. Even with these reductions, the Air Force can only fill 96 percent of fighter pilot requirements at operational units. The Air Force is implementing additional initiatives to mitigate shortages on staffs, deployed positions, and in the training enterprise. Voluntary return to active duty programs allow members of the Air Reserve Component to fill staff and training positions. Additionally, the Air Force is exploring opportunities for Air Reserve Component members to volunteer for 179- and 365-day deployments.

MITIGATION EFFORTS – INCREASED PILOT PRODUCTION

The Air Force recognizes the need to increase pilot production and has taken steps to expand Undergraduate Pilot Training to maximum training capacity. However, sufficient manpower, infrastructure, and operations and maintenance resources would be needed to support any future increase in throughput. The Air Force is actively pursuing additional ways to increase production across the entire training pipeline to mission-ready status. This includes creating two new F-16 Formal Training Units, increasing the number of total force active-associate units, leveraging opportunities to increase active duty fighter pilot absorption at Air National Guard (ANG) fighter units, and exploring a specific helicoptor track for undergraduate pilot training to increase capacity for fixed wing pilots.

The Air Force appreciates Congress authorizing and funding an increase in active-duty end-strength to 321,000 for FY17. This essential growth enables the Air Force to train and develop new pilots and maintain legacy aircraft longer than before. This immediate end-strength increase is vital. The Air Force will consider end-strength increases as it works with the Secretary of Defense to develop the Fiscal Year's 2018 President's Budget request. Further, we must retain these newly trained Airmen.

MITIGATION EFFORTS – INCREASED RETENTION

Given the American taxpayer investment and the substantial time required to train and season an Air Force pilot, it is vital that our nation retains this talent. The Air Force employs a variety of monetary and non-monetary force management initiatives to produce the right mix and number of experienced Airmen. The Air Force will implement the first increase in the Aviation Bonus in 18 years. A tiered business case analysis model identifies areas of greatest need, and our pilots who continue to serve beyond their initial service commitment will receive up to $35,000 per year, authorized by the FY17 NDAA. Air Force is also considering incentives for hard to fill assignments where many Airmen choose to separate from service rather than accepting the position.

Retaining our pilot force goes beyond financial incentives…it's about culture. The Air Force is implementing many non-monetary efforts to strengthen the culture and improve the quality of life and quality of service for our Airmen. We reduced additional duties, removed non-mission-essential training courses and outsourced select routine administrative tasks. All of these efforts allow our pilots to focus on their primary duty: flying.

We increased the transparency and flexibility of the assignment process to promote family stability. We are also exploring options that allow active duty pilots to work for the civilian aviation industry through the Career Intermission Program and then return to the active force upon completion of that intermission.

BOLD INITIATIVES

But we are not stopping at these mitigation efforts. The Air Force is aggressively pursuing bold initiatives to address the shortfalls in pilot manning and stabilize the inventory over the long term. Restructuring retention packages and making fundamental changes to how we manage our Airmen will take time. But our goal with these long-term solutions is to set the conditions for the Air Force to regain and maintain a full-spectrum, mission-ready force in support of the National Military Strategy.

We know based on exit survey data that not all pilots separate from the Air Force for the same reason. Therefore, the Air Force must divest a "one size fits all" retention model, and we should tailor retention packages to the individual Airman from a host of options. This could include a traditional financial bonus, or it could include other incentives like preferential basing, longer timelines between required Permanent Changes of Station (PCS), or methods for deployment relief. In any case, Airmen can choose a retention package that fits their current needs.

Maintaining a work/life balance and meeting family commitments is paramount to our servicemembers. When the Officer Personnel Act was passed in 1947, only 25 percent of married couples with children had two income earners. Today, that number is over 60 percent. Moving families every 2-3 years makes it difficult for spouses to pursue and maintain a career. The way we relocate our Airmen must keep pace with today's family, or we will lose talent.

Additionally, our Airmen deserve an updated assignment system that can meet manning requirements as well as ensure mission success. Therefore, a beta test is currently underway that could change how we execute assignments. This test involves the use of algorithms to optimize assignments based on the needs of the Air Force and desires of our members and their families—an assignment system for the 21st century.

In the past, the Air Force used warrant officers for mission sets that required technical proficiency. While reinstituting this model is not an impossible option, other courses of action may deliver the same desired result in a much shorter timeline. The Air Force will examine possible alternate career paths for pilots. A tailored number of our pilot force could diverge from the current "up-or-out" career progression model into a technical, non-command career track. This would allow them to remain in service while focusing principally on flying duties. This would retain valuable talent and keep credible instructors in operational squadrons and schoolhouses where they are needed most.

<u>CONCLUSION</u>

The Air Force is committed to a holistic strategy to maintain our pilot inventory by reducing requirements, increasing pilot production, and improving retention through bold monetary and non-monetary programs. While we aggressively pursue creative means to respond to the demands on our pilots, our attention will be focused on developing an agile set of solutions and will not hesitate to seek the Congress' support for revised or new authorities and resources in the future. We appreciate your support as we face this national crisis for our most valuable resource, our talented Airmen, and believe our actions should be bold and decisive to retain a group core to our identity.

Lieutenant General Gina M. Grosso

Lt. Gen. Gina M. Grosso is the Deputy Chief of Staff for Manpower, Personnel and Services, Headquarters U.S. Air Force, Washington, D.C. General Grosso serves as the senior Air Force officer responsible for comprehensive plans and policies covering all life cycles of military and civilian personnel management, which includes military and civilian end strength management, education and training, compensation, resource allocation, and the worldwide U.S. Air Force services program.

General Grosso entered the Air Force in 1986 as a Reserve Officer Training Corps distinguished graduate from Carnegie-Mellon University, Pittsburgh, Pennsylvania. She has held several command and staff positions throughout her career. As a staff officer, she served as an operations analyst, personnel programs analyst, Air Staff and Office of the Secretary of Defense action officer, Major Command Director of Manpower and Personnel, Director of the Air Force Colonel Management Office, Director, Manpower, Organization and Resources, and Director of Force Management Policy. Her command tours include a Headquarters Squadron Section, Military Personnel Flight, Mission Support Squadron, command of the Air Force's sole Basic Military Training Group, and as Joint Base and 87th Air Base Wing commander at Joint Base McGuire-Dix-Lakehurst, NJ. Prior to her current assignment, she was the Director of the Air Force Sexual Assault Prevention and Response (SAPR), Office of the Vice Chief of Staff, Headquarters U.S. Air Force, Washington, D.C.

EDUCATION
1986 Bachelor of Science, Applied Mathematics and Industrial Management, Carnegie-Mellon University, Pittsburgh, Pa.
1992 Master's degree in business administration, College of William and Mary, Williamsburg, Va.
1993 Squadron Officer School, Maxwell AFB, Ala.
1997 Air Command and Staff College, Seminar
1999 Master's degree in national security and strategic studies, Naval Command and Staff College, Newport, R.I.
2000 Air War College, Seminar
2004 Fellow, Weatherhead Center for International Affairs, Harvard University, Boston, Mass.

ASSIGNMENTS
1. October 1986 - October 1988, Operations Analyst, followed by Commander, Headquarters Squadron Section, 554th Range Group, Nellis AFB, Nev.
2. November 1988 - April 1992, Personnel Programs and Force Programs Analyst, Deputy Chief of Staff, Personnel, Headquarters Tactical Air Command, Langley AFB, Va.
3. May 1992 - May 1993, Executive Officer, Directorate of Personnel, Headquarters Air Combat Command, Langley AFB, Va.
4. May 1993 - July 1993, Student, Squadron Officer School, Maxwell AFB, Ala.
5. August 1993 - May 1995, Commander, Military Personnel Flight, 6th Mission Support Squadron, MacDill AFB, Fla.
6. June 1995 - January 1997, Chief, Personnel Policy, followed by Deputy Chief, Support Division, Air Force Colonel Matters Office, Pentagon, Washington D.C.
7. January 1997 - July 1998, Member, Chief of Staff of the Air Force Operations Group, Headquarters Air Force, Pentagon, Washington D.C.
8. July 1998 - July 1999, Student, Naval Command and Staff College, Newport, R.I.
9. July 1999 - July 2001, Commander, 51st Mission Support Squadron, Osan Air Base, South Korea
10. July 2001 - May 2002, Assistant Director, Enlisted Plans and Policy, Office of the Secretary of Defense, the Pentagon, Washington D.C.

11. May 2002 - July 2003, Military Assistant, Deputy Under Secretary of Defense for Military Personnel Policy, Pentagon, Washington D.C.
12. July 2003 - July 2004, Fellow, Weatherhead Center for International Affairs, Harvard University, Boston, Mass.
13. July 2004 - July 2006, Commander, 737th Training Group, Lackland AFB, Texas
14. July 2006 - July 2007, Director, Manpower and Personnel, Headquarters Pacific Air Forces, Hickam AFB, Hawaii
15. July 2007 - March 2009, Director, Air Force Colonels Management Office, the Pentagon, Washington D.C.
16. March 2009 - June 2011, Commander, Joint Base and 87th Air Base Wing, Joint Base McGuire-Dix-Lakehurst, N.J.
17. June 2011 - August 2012, Director, Manpower, Organization and Resources, the Pentagon, Washington D.C.
18. August 2012 - January 2014, Director, Force Management Policy, the Pentagon, Washington D.C.
19. February 2014 - October 2015, Director, Air Force Sexual Assault Prevention and Response Office, Office of the Vice Chief of Staff, Headquarters U.S. Air Force, Washington, D.C.
20. October 2015 - present, Deputy Chief of Staff, Manpower, Personnel and Services, Headquarters U.S. Air Force, Washington D.C.

SUMMARY OF JOINT ASSIGNMENTS

1. July 2001 - May 2002, Assistant Director, Enlisted Plans and Policy, Office of the Secretary of Defense, Pentagon, Washington D.C., as a lieutenant colonel
2. May 2002 - July 2003, Military Assistant, Deputy Under Secretary of Defense for Military Personnel Policy, Pentagon, Washington D.C., as a lieutenant colonel
3. March 2009 - June 2011, Commander, Joint Base and 87th Air Base Wing, Joint Base McGuire-Dix-Lakehurst, N.J., as a colonel and brigadier general

MAJOR AWARDS AND DECORATIONS

Defense Superior Service Medal
Legion of Merit with two oak leaf cluster
Meritorious Service Medal with three oak leaf clusters
Army Commendation Medal
Air Force Commendation Medal
Joint Service Achievement Medal
Air Force Achievement Medal with one oak leaf cluster
Air Force Outstanding Unit Award with one oak leaf cluster
Air Force Organizational Excellence Award with three oak leaf clusters
National Defense Service Medal with bronze star
Global War on Terrorism Medal
Korean Defense Service Medal
Humanitarian Service Medal

OTHER ACHIEVMENTS

Tactical Air Command, Deputy Chief of Staff, Personnel, 1990 CGO of the Year
Tactical Air Command, 1991 Junior Personnel Manager of the Year
Distinguished Graduate, Squadron Officer School, 1993
6th Air Base Wing Lance P. Sijan Leadership Award, Junior Officer Category for 1995
Headquarters Air Force, Senior Personnel Manager of the Year for 1996

EFFECTIVE DATES OF PROMOTION

Second Lieutenant Oct. 2, 1986
First Lieutenant July 17, 1988
Captain July 17, 1990
Major Aug. 1, 1996
Lieutenant Colonel July 1, 1999

Colonel Aug. 1, 2003
Brigadier General April 1, 2011
Major General July 24, 2014
Lieutenant General Oct. 15, 2015

(Current as of October 2015)

RECORD VERSION

STATEMENT BY

**MAJOR GENERAL ERIK C. PETERSON
DIRECTOR OF ARMY AVIATION,
DEPUTY CHIEF OF STAFF G-3/5/7**

BEFORE THE

**HOUSE ARMED SERVICES COMMITTEE
SUBCOMMITTEE ON MILITARY PERSONNEL**

FIRST SESSION, 115TH CONGRESS

ON ARMY PILOT SHORTAGES AND STRATEGIES TO MITIGATE

MARCH 29, 2017

**NOT FOR PUBLICATION UNTIL RELEASED BY THE
COMMITTEE ON ARMED SERVICES**

STATEMENT BY
MAJOR GENERAL ERIK C. PETERSON
DIRECTOR OF ARMY AVIATION,
DEPUTY CHIEF OF STAFF G-3/5/7

Chairman Coffman, Ranking Member Speier, and distinguished Members of the Subcommittee on Military Personnel, I appreciate the opportunity to appear before you to discuss the state of Army Aviation pilot shortages and our Army's mitigation strategy.

The Total Army Force consisting of the Regular Army, the Army National Guard (ARNG), and the Army Reserve (USAR) employs over 4,000 total aircraft in its inventory, including both fixed- and rotary-wing (and an additional 8,000 unmanned systems). Those aircraft are expertly operated by approximately 14,000 rated aviators (and an additional 1,600 active component unmanned operators) across all three components. These Soldiers are operating in 39 countries around the world executing combat and theater security cooperation missions, while the remainder operate and train across all 54 States and Territories, building decisive action readiness and meeting domestic mission requirements.

Army Aviation provides an asymmetric advantage for our Nation as a combat multiplier. We remain focused on ensuring Combatant Commanders and our joint and coalition partners have the required reach, protection, lethality and situational understanding to win in an increasingly complex world, in exceptionally challenging conditions. The distinct advantage that Army Aviation provides is built on a foundation of highly trained and professional Army Aviation leaders and Soldiers.

For nearly 16 years, Army Aviation has been tested in the most demanding of operational environments at an unprecedented pace and duration, and our Soldiers and leaders have performed magnificently. Nevertheless, force structure adjustments and fiscal constraints caused the Army to make very difficult resourcing choices. We prioritized short-term readiness over the long-term recruiting and training required to achieve a strong, healthy force. We simply could not afford to train the number of pilots we needed to sustain a fully manned, healthy force. More importantly, the current pilot strength across our force masks long-term pilot challenges that lie ahead.

Background

In response to a changing fiscal environment, and as a direct result of the implementation of the Budget Control Act of 2011, programmed training allocations were set below the minimum requirement. Due to these allocation shortfalls, there is a significant inventory gap in Regular Army Aviation Warrant Officers commissioned between 2010-2017. Additionally, more recent challenges with training throughput and civilian hiring competition for aviators further exacerbates the deficit. Although current pilot fill rates in our Regular Army Combat Aviation Brigades remain acceptable in all but the Apache fleet, the Army accessed 731 fewer Regular Army Warrant Officers over the past seven years than required to maintain a healthy force in the long term. We are currently achieving marginally acceptable manning by relying on senior Aviation Warrant Officers serving in junior positions. Simply put – in the short term, we are "top heavy" in compensating for our current accession and training deficit. Solutions we apply, however creative, will help but will not make up for several years of lost opportunity to recruit, access and train the right number of aviators. Although substantial shortages have not yet materialized in the Reserve Components; without deliberate action, shortfalls can be expected across the Total Army Force.

A recent development that compounds this problem is the active recruitment of Army helicopter pilots by the airline industry. From a historical perspective, the draw on military rotary-wing pilots by the major airlines has been relatively low. However, as the senior commercial airline pilots age and retire from the major airlines, the demand for replacement pilots has outpaced supply. As a result of this demand, major airlines have adjusted their entry requirements to facilitate an aggressive recruiting campaign for military rotary-wing pilots. Although this campaign is in its infancy, the new airline entry requirements allow a much larger portion of Army pilots to join, and when coupled with enticing monetary incentives, will undoubtedly challenge the Army's ability to maintain a healthy and highly-skilled aviation force in all components.

Current Efforts and Way Forward

The Army is addressing the challenge of Aviation Warrant Officer shortages and will build long-term readiness through closely managed and simultaneous resourcing, equipping, and training strategies, while managing risk to aviation readiness across the Army. To accomplish this, we are focusing on three lines of effort: retention, training throughput, and accessions.

Retention of highly competent aviators is key to mitigating personnel shortages while the Army produces additional aviators to fill those shortages. Although retention across the Army is healthy, we have seen a steady increase in attrition of Aviation Warrant Officers over the last three years. Aviation Warrant Officer attrition rates have historically been around seven percent over the last decade but are now approaching nine percent. This trend is expected to continue unless we take swift action. Over 25% of these Aviation Warrant Officers are retirement eligible, with increasingly attractive opportunities in the civilian market. A growing shortage of mid-grade pilots available to replace the retirement eligible pilots further complicates the problem until a sufficient level of flight school graduates are able to mature within the pilot inventory to offset current shortages. These factors cause the Army to move pilots from one unit to another to meet deployment requirements, reducing dwell time and potentially intensifying the problem. To address retention issues the Army is formalizing graduated incentives that encourage pilots to continue their military aviation career as well as further rewarding pilots who advance their aviation qualifications. Attrition analysis indicates two key areas to target for retention incentives: pilots nearing the end of their six year Active Duty Service Obligation (ADSO) and retirement eligible Warrant Officers. Incentives under evaluation include Assignment Incentive Pay (AIP), Aviation Bonus (AvB) pay, and additional incentive pay for specialized qualifications (i.e. Instructor Pilot and Maintenance Test Pilot).

Additionally, the Army is increasing its capacity to train new pilots to ensure adequate inventories in the future. This commitment to fully resourcing our flight school is not a quick fix and must be phased in over several years. The Army plans to budget at a higher level than in the past to be successful. The United States Army Aviation Center of Excellence (USAACE) at Fort Rucker, Alabama provides world-class aviation training. Maintaining high standards for training is critical to ensure the aviation force is ready to meet mission requirements and reduces risk. To achieve the appropriate number of trained pilots to support 23 Aviation Brigades (11 Active Component, 10 Army National Guard and 2 Army Reserve), the Army requires the training base to operate at near maximum capacity. Core requirements to meet this capacity include Initial Entry Rotary Wing (IERW) training as well as graduate level training to support production of instructor pilots and maintenance test pilots. The Army must carefully balance these core requirements with an increasing demand for training in support of Foreign Military Sales (FMS) and requests for training from sister services. While the Army must maintain our commitments with sister services and foreign partners, we have an obligation to place increased priority on mitigating our growing shortages first.

As the Army provides additional resources to its training base, we will also synchronize an incremental increase to Regular Army Warrant Officer accessions to deliberately grow our throughput to meet operational demand and correct for previous under accessions. Over the next three years, the Army will increase Regular Army Aviation Warrant Officer throughput by nearly 170 students. Maintaining the proper level of accessions of both Commissioned and Warrant Officers across all components is critical to the sustainment of 23 Aviation Brigades in the Total Army. Processes for analyzing and adjusting accession levels must also remain flexible to allow for future end state growth as operational requirements evolve.

Specifically, the Army is implementing nine strategies outlined below to overcome these shortfalls, and plans to budget at a higher level of resourcing than it has in the past, to fully implement. We already see positive change to throughput with consistent reductions to training backlog without jeopardizing the quality of pilots produced:

- Increase accessions from a planned 308 in Fiscal Year 2017 to 475 Regular Army Aviation Warrant Officers over the next 2-3 years.

- Offer graduated incentives and promotion opportunity that encourage pilots to continue their military aviation career as well as further rewarding pilots who advance their aviation qualifications.
- Actively recruit AH-64 and CH-47 qualified pilots who have recently left service. Leadership will assess aviators from this population for qualifications that would allow select personnel to augment training cadre at flight school.
- Look across the Total Army to leverage experience from aviators in our Reserve Components at the training base without negatively impacting Reserve Component units.
- Augment training base with higher instructor pilot fill rates through Call to Active Duty, Retiree Recall, and Active Duty Operational Support.
- Augment training base with aircraft (AH-64E and CH-47F), simulation devices, and instructor pilots.
- Adjust Program of Instruction (POI) to gain efficiencies where possible without reducing quality of training.
- Establish a Mobile Training Team to conduct AH-64D Aircraft Qualification Courses at unit Home Station (conversion of unit from OH-58D to AH-64D).
- Provide maintenance augmentation by operational units in support of training base as operational requirements allow.

Conclusion

As we focus on the future, the Army is taking steps to maximize Total Army Aviation Training capacity to meet current requirements while anticipating future growth. Though the Army currently possesses sufficient authorities to support increased accession and improved retention within assumed top-line budget projections, it is important that we are provided consistent budgetary support at our request levels to avoid shortfalls of the past. We can assure you that the Army's senior leaders are working to address current manning challenges, as well as the needs of the Army to provide capability anywhere, any time, against any threat.

Mr. Chairman and distinguished Members of this Subcommittee, thank you for your steadfast support of the outstanding men and women in uniform, our Army Civilians, and their Families.

 United States Army

Major General ERIK C. PETERSON

Director, Army Aviation
Office of the Deputy Chief of Staff, G-3/5/7
United States Army
450 Army Pentagon 3A474
Washington, DC 20310-0450
Since: August 2016

SOURCE OF COMMISSIONED SERVICE ROTC

EDUCATIONAL DEGREES
University of Idaho – BS – Geography
University of Idaho – BS – Cartography
Touro College, New York – MBA – Business Administration
National Defense University – MS – National Security and Strategic Studies

MILITARY SCHOOLS ATTENDED
Aviation Officer Basic and Advanced Courses
United States Army Command and General Staff College
National War College

FOREIGN LANGUAGE(S) None recorded

PROMOTIONS	DATE OF APPOINTMENT
2LT	17 May 86
1LT	28 Nov 87
CPT	1 Sep 90
MAJ	1 Mar 97
LTC	1 Jun 01
COL	1 Dec 06
BG	2 May 13
MG	2 Jul 16

FROM	TO	ASSIGNMENT
Aug 16	Present	Director, Army Aviation, Office of the Deputy Chief of Staff, G-3/5/7, United States Army, Washington, DC
Jun 14	Jul 16	Commanding General, United States Army Special Operations Aviation Command, Fort Bragg, North Carolina
Jun 13	Jun 14	Deputy Commanding General (Support), 2d Infantry Division, Eighth United States Army, Republic of Korea
Aug 12	May 13	Deputy Commanding General, United States Army Cadet Command, Fort Knox, Kentucky
Nov 09	Jul 12	Chief of Staff, 10th Mountain Division (Light Infantry), Fort Drum, New York and Combined Joint Task Force-10/Regional Command-South, OPERATION ENDURING FREEDOM, Afghanistan
Aug 07	Nov 09	Commander, 10th Combat Aviation Brigade, Fort Drum, New York and OPERATION IRAQI FREEDOM, Iraq
Aug 06	Jun 07	Student, National War College, Washington, DC
Jul 04	Aug 06	Director, Flight Concepts Division, Fort Eustis, Virginia and OPERATION IRAQI FREEDOM, Iraq and OPERATION ENDURING FREEDOM, Afghanistan
Jun 02	Jul 04	Commander, 2d Battalion, 160th Special Operations Aviation Regiment (Airborne), Fort Campbell, Kentucky and OPERATION ENDURING FREEDOM, Afghanistan
Mar 01	Mar 02	Senior Special Operations Aviation Observer/Controller, Joint Readiness Training Center Operations Group, Fort Polk, Louisiana
Jun 98	Mar 01	Executive Officer, later Commander, B Company, 3d Battalion, 160th Special Operations Aviation Regiment (Airborne), Hunter Army Airfield, Georgia
Jun 97	Jun 98	Student, United States Army Command and General Staff Officer Course, Fort Leavenworth, Kansas
Mar 94	Jun 97	Adjutant, later Operations Officer, 2d Battalion, 160th Special Operations Aviation Regiment (Airborne), Fort Campbell, Kentucky and OPERATION UPHOLD DEMOCRACY, Haiti
Jul 93	Mar 94	Student, Aviation Officer Advanced Course, United States Aviation Center, Fort Rucker, Alabama

Dec 88 Jul 93 Commander, later Platoon Leader, B Company, later Commander, Headquarters and Headquarters Company, 3d Battalion, 160th Special Operations Aviation Regiment (Airborne), Hunter Army Airfield, Georgia and OPERATION DESERT STORM, Saudi Arabia

Jul 87 Dec 88 Section Leader, later Platoon Leader, 271st Combat Aviation Company, 17th Aviation Brigade, Republic of Korea

SUMMARY OF JOINT ASSIGNMENTS	DATE	GRADE
Chief of Staff, 10th Mountain Division (Light Infantry), Combined Joint Task Force-10/Regional Command-South, OPERATION ENDURING FREEDOM, Afghanistan	Sep 10 - Oct 11	Colonel
Commander, 2d Battalion, 160th Special Operations Aviation Regiment (Airborne), OPERATION ENDURING FREEDOM, Afghanistan	Apr 03 - Apr 04	Lieutenant Colonel

SUMMARY OF OPERATIONAL ASSIGNMENTS	DATE	GRADE
Chief of Staff, 10th Mountain Division (Light Infantry), Combined Joint Task Force-10/Regional Command-South, OPERATION ENDURING FREEDOM, Afghanistan	Sep 10 - Oct 11	Colonel
Commander, 10th Combat Aviation Brigade, Fort Drum, New York and OPERATION IRAQI FREEDOM, Iraq	Oct 08 - Oct 09	Colonel
Director, Flight Concepts Division, Fort Eustis, Virginia and OPERATION IRAQI FREEDOM, Iraq	Nov 05 - Apr 06	Lieutenant Colonel
Director, Flight Concepts Division, Fort Eustis, Virginia and OPERATION ENDURING FREEDOM, Afghanistan	Apr 05 - Jun 05	Lieutenant Colonel
Commander, 2d Battalion, 160th Special Operations Aviation Regiment (Airborne), OPERATION ENDURING FREEDOM, Afghanistan	Apr 03 - Apr 04	Lieutenant Colonel
Adjutant, later S-3, 2d Battalion, 160th Special Operations Aviation Regiment (Airborne), Fort Campbell, Kentucky and OPERATION UPHOLD DEMOCRACY, Haiti	Oct 94 - Nov 94	Captain
Commander, later Platoon Leader, B Company, later Commander, Headquarters and Headquarters Company, 3d Battalion, 160th Special Operations Aviation Regiment (Airborne), Hunter Army Airfield, Georgia and OPERATION DESERT STORM, Saudi Arabia	Nov 90 - Apr 91	Captain

US DECORATIONS AND BADGES
Distinguished Service Medal
Legion of Merit (with 3 Bronze Oak Leaf Clusters)
Bronze Star Medal (with Silver Oak Leaf Cluster)
Meritorious Service Medal (with 4 Bronze Oak Leaf Clusters)
Air Medal for Valor
Air Medal (Numeral 4)
Army Commendation Medal (with 1 Bronze Oak Leaf Cluster)
Army Achievement Medal (with 1 Bronze Oak Leaf Cluster)
Combat Action Badge
Master Parachutist Badge
Air Assault Badge
Master Army Aviator Badge

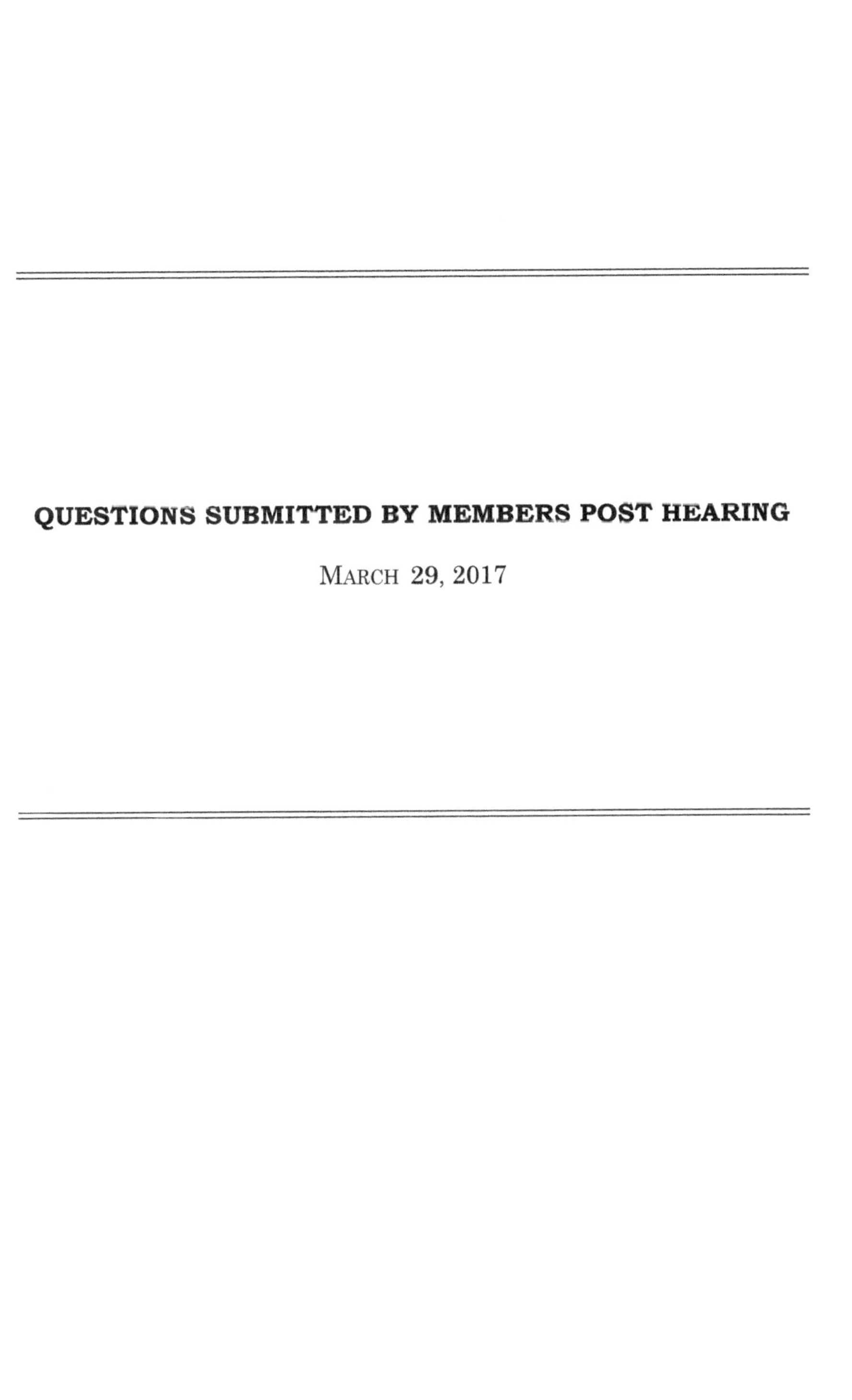
QUESTIONS SUBMITTED BY MEMBERS POST HEARING

MARCH 29, 2017

Ms. SPEIER. In my opening statement, I discussed the importance of understanding the real reasons that pilots leave the service, which are often non-monetary. If a pilot is not happy with their assignments or deployment schedules, all the money in the world may not be able to keep them in the service. Given these issues, can each of you briefly explain how you are employing non-monetary incentives to retain pilots?

General BRILAKIS. The Marine Corps works individually with officers to try and match their personal preferences with suitable requirements in the operating force which may positively influence an individual's decision to remain, vice resign. Duty station preference, unit preference, time on station waivers, geo-location preference, and assignments outside of their primary occupation are areas we look at to incentivize the retention of aviators, while also filling mission critical requirements.

Ms. SPEIER. In my opening statement, I discussed the importance of understanding the real reasons that pilots leave the service, which are often non-monetary. If a pilot is not happy with their assignments or deployment schedules, all the money in the world may not be able to keep them in the service. Given these issues, can each of you briefly explain how you are employing non-monetary incentives to retain pilots?

Admiral BURKE. Career exit surveys indicate a number of complex, inter-related factors leading to pilot decisions to leave service, including an improving economy with increasing opportunities for commercial airline industry employment. Aviators also express dissatisfaction in their quality of service due to readiness challenges associated with limited aircraft availability (number of airframes and lack of spare parts), reduced flying hours, timely attainment of tactical qualifications and career progression, frequency of moves, and deployment lengths/time away from family. Non-monetary retention incentives have focused on improving quality of service and work-life balance through increased choice and flexibility in a successful career path. While relatively new, we are seeing progress through initiatives such as the Career Intermission Program (CIP), increased graduate education options, opportunities for Tours with Industry (TWI), the High School Senior Stability initiative, and efforts to incorporate personnel management process changes as part of Sailor 2025. Increasing numbers of aviation officers are taking advantage of CIP, which affords them a one-three year sabbatical for various reasons, such as starting a family, furthering education, or fulfilling other ambitions that might otherwise have caused them to leave the Navy. After intermission, they return to service without harm to their career progression or competitiveness. The intent of TWI is to familiarize a cadre of Sailors with corporate planning, organization, management techniques, innovations, and best practices by placing them with leading private sector corporations for one year. The experience enhances their professional development and better prepares them for follow-on Navy tours, during which their new skills can be leveraged. Under the High School Senior Stability initiative, when a dependent family member enters their junior year of high school, the Sailor may submit a request to remain in the same geographic location to permit the dependent to complete their senior year of high school. Such career broadening measures, aimed at increasing career flexibility, experience and choice, when coupled with judicious applications of monetary incentives, are key to improving aviation retention in the long term.

Ms. SPEIER. Congress increased the aviation bonus from $25,000 to $35,000 in the FY17 NDAA. Vice Admiral Burke and LTG Grosso: does this amount provide enough flexibility to use higher bonuses to retain the most critical skills, while also providing the rest of the pilots with a lower incentive?

Admiral BURKE. End-strength and pilot production levels are not directly contributing to aviation retention challenges, thus neither is expected to improve near-term retention. While we are accessing and training sufficient numbers of pilots to meet requirements, mid-grade and senior pilots in some communities, such as Strike Fighter (VFA), Electronic Attack (VAQ) and Mine Warfare (HM), are leaving the Navy at higher-than-expected rates, challenging our ability to meet subsequent flying and non-flying assignment requirements. Aviation accessions are based on an annual demand to fill first fleet squadron billets with junior officers who replace incumbents vacating billets for routine tour rotations/progression. Retention rates of aviators after the first tour have historically proven sufficient in the aggregate to meet manning and selectivity requirements for subsequent career milestone billets—such as department head and command—and the many sea shore billets the aviation community fills. Annual aviation accessions of around 1,000–1,100 annually, since 2012, coupled with our ability to train accessions on time, has provided a sustainable model, as long as retention goals were being met. Today's retention challenges, in some communities, are occurring between the 10 and 20-year service points. While end-strength increases may eventually yield larger accession year groups that could equate to larger overall pilot inventories, increasing populations beyond that needed for immediate first fleet squadron billets would take over 10 years. Also, while increasing pilot production could generate more pilots for first fleet sea tours in the near term, creating excess populations in some fleet squadrons, this cadre could still choose to resign at the end of their initial minimum service requirement, prior to serving a critical department head tour, so the increase would not necessarily resolve the retention challenges we face today.

Ms. SPEIER. In my opening statement, I discussed the importance of understanding the real reasons that pilots leave the service, which are often non-monetary. If a pilot is not happy with their assignments or deployment schedules, all the money in the world may not be able to keep them in the service. Given these issues, can each of you briefly explain how you are employing non-monetary incentives to retain pilots?

General GROSSO. The AF is employing several non-monetary incentives to improve pilot retention, to include increased assignment and development education flexibility, and removing dozens of non-flying additional duties and computer based training modules from their workload. Arguably, the most meaningful non-monetary incentive for pilot retention has been the addition of civilian contractors in flying squadrons to assist with laborious non-flying tasks required for day-to-day flight operations. These individuals allow pilots to spend more time studying, flying, and learning how to be the best in the world at what they do. Although ACC is currently the only MAJCOM to have assigned admin contractors, PACAF, AETC, USAFE, and AFGSC should also have contractors in place by the spring of 2018. Additionally, increasing end-strength numbers will certainly help with the pilot shortage as many of those members will be maintenance personnel tasked with keeping old aircraft flying and flying is what our pilots want to do. Furthermore, AETC's maximum available pilot production is ~1,400 per year due to available runways, daylight and training ranges. The Air Force must develop additional training capacity in order to increase production to 1,600 pilots annually, the amount we will need to sustain 60 fighter squadrons and mitigate pending shortfalls in other platforms.

Ms. SPEIER. Congress increased the aviation bonus from $25,000 to $35,000 in the FY17 NDAA. Vice Admiral Burke and LTG Grosso: does this amount provide enough flexibility to use higher bonuses to retain the most critical skills, while also providing the rest of the pilots with a lower incentive?

General GROSSO. The Air Force appreciates the $35,000 annual cap authorized in the FY17 NDAA. The Air Force will use the FY17 NDAA Aviation Bonus authority and implement using a business case model to identify areas of greatest need. The business case model will be run annually and consider manning levels (current and trend), retention levels (current and trend), timeline for generating replacements, and costs to train/generate replacements. However, based on the RAND study directed by the FY16 NDAA, we believe the $35,000 cap limits the Services' ability to retain pilots in our most critical need area (Fighter Pilots), but also limits the Services' ability to retain aviators in areas of lesser need. The RAND study suggested a higher bonus authority was needed to incentivize the retention levels required to maintain our pilot force. We will analyze the effectiveness of our FY17 Aviation Bonus program under current authorities and then may need additional support in the form of increased authority to include an increased Aviation Bonus ceiling.

Ms. SPEIER. In my opening statement, I discussed the importance of understanding the real reasons that pilots leave the service, which are often non-monetary. If a pilot is not happy with their assignments or deployment schedules, all the money in the world may not be able to keep them in the service. Given these issues, can each of you briefly explain how you are employing non-monetary incentives to retain pilots?

General PETERSON. Although retention across Army Aviation is not an immediate problem, recent trends indicate the need for increased focus on Aviation Warrant Officer incentives. Retention of highly competent aviators is key to mitigating current personnel shortages while the Army produces additional aviators to fill those shortages. The Army is unique in that the preponderance of our Rated Aviators are

Warrant Officers. This allows, by design, the career paths of Aviation Warrant Officers to focus on pilot related duties and advancement through specialized pilot training, with minimal requirements to serve in assignments outside of Aviation. The primary incentive for an Army Aviator to remain in service will always be the opportunity to develop within their craft and seek advanced pilot and leadership positions. The Army encourages and supports this endeavor by offering other incentives to assist the aviator both personally and professionally. Two opportunities available to Aviation Warrant Officers are the Degree Completion Program and Broadening Assignments such as Flight School Instructors and Training Center Observers. Both of these opportunities allow Warrant Officers a break from the high Operational Tempo that is common within Army Aviation units, as well as the opportunity to either complete their educational goals or to develop their tactical and technical warfighting skills. It is also an important goal for the Army to provide not only aviators, but all Soldiers, the ability to be assigned to personally desirable duty stations for a duration that allows predictability for the Soldier and their family. Our human resources personnel carefully manage this important consideration based on Soldier preferences and operational and institutional requirements. As current shortages are mitigated and manning levels improve, the Army will have better capacity to meet these goals. The Army is exploring all options to enhance the current programs available and institute additional programs into policy. There are opportunities within the Degree Completion and Broadening Assignments to expand the current target population providing more access to the programs. The Army will also continue to emphasize assignment stability within its ability to meet our Country's operational requirements. Critical to the success of any current or future program is the health of our current force. Manning shortages limit opportunities for aviators to serve in broadening or educational assignments based on requirements to man aircraft and units in support of Army requirements at home and abroad. Fixing current manning shortages will allow for these opportunities in the future and help to stabilize our Total Force.

____

QUESTIONS SUBMITTED BY MS. ROSEN

Ms. ROSEN. What parts of the personnel system (for example, assignments or promotions) do you assess must be changed to aid in retention?

Admiral BURKE. Through Sailor 2025, Navy is pursuing a dynamic set of approximately 45 non-monetary initiatives designed to improve retention across the force. Built on a framework of three pillars—a modernized personnel system, ready relevant learning, and career readiness—Sailor 2025 is a roadmap designed to change our approach to personnel programs by providing Sailors with choice and flexibility. These initiatives target modernizing personnel management and training systems to more-effectively find, recruit, train, and manage the careers of, talented people, thus improving retention and warfighting readiness. For example, we are modernizing Navy's fitness reporting and evaluation system, increasing emphasis on merit-based pay incentives, and continuing efforts to improve the transparency and accessibility of our detailing system/process for Sailors and their families. While existing statutory authorities provide the necessary tools to adequately influence current aviator retention behavior, we continually assess the sufficiency and effectiveness of our efforts to enable efficient retention, and when needed, recommend changes to provide the tools and flexibility needed to meet emerging demand.

Ms. ROSEN. Will the end-strength increases in the FY 17 NDAA help with the shortage, or are there other physical barriers to increasing pilot production such as school-house size or instructor cadre?

Admiral BURKE. End-strength and pilot production levels are not directly contributing to aviation retention challenges, thus neither is expected to improve near-term retention. While we are accessing and training sufficient numbers of pilots to meet requirements, mid-grade and senior pilots in some communities, such as Strike Fighter (VFA), Electronic Attack (VAQ) and Mine Warfare (HM), are leaving the Navy at higher-than-expected rates, challenging our ability to meet subsequent flying and non-flying assignment requirements. Aviation accessions are based on an annual demand to fill first fleet squadron billets with junior officers who replace incumbents vacating billets for routine tour rotations/progression. Retention rates of aviators after the first tour have historically proven sufficient in the aggregate to meet manning and selectivity requirements for subsequent career milestone billets—such as department head and command—and the many sea shore billets the aviation community fills. Annual aviation accessions of around 1,000–1,100 annually, since 2012, coupled with our ability to train accessions on time, has provided a sustainable model, as long as retention goals were being met. Today's retention challenges, in some communities, are occurring between the 10 and 20-year service points. While end-strength increases may eventually yield larger accession year groups that could equate to larger overall pilot inventories, increasing populations beyond that needed for immediate first fleet squadron billets would take over 10 years. Also, while increasing pilot production could generate more pilots for first fleet sea tours in the near term, creating excess populations in some fleet squadrons, this cadre could still choose to resign at the end of their initial minimum service requirement, prior to serving a critical department head tour, so the increase would not necessarily resolve the retention challenges we face today.

Ms. ROSEN. Since flight hours are a motivator for retention, is your aircraft force structure robust and healthy enough to support all of your minimum required pilot flying hours? Will you be able to increase flying time with an increased budget or will it require more airplanes?

Admiral BURKE. The aircraft force structure is not currently adequate to fulfill the minimum number of required flying hours to establish and maintain optimum aviation readiness. Available funding must be spread over a number of priorities, including depot capacity, readiness accounts—particularly those that buy/sustain the supply of aircraft parts—and procurement. Shortfalls in each of these areas impose risk in meeting both minimum flight hour requirements as well as current and future Global Force Management (GFM) operational commitments. While investments in the President's fiscal year 2017 budget begin to address the gap between strike fighter inventory and GFM demand by fully funding depot capacity, consistent long-term investments will be essential to fully-funding flying hours, enabling depot operations, making readiness and supply accounts whole, and procuring replacement aircraft at a rate that outpaces consumption.

Ms. ROSEN. I am deeply concerned with how pilot shortfalls are impacting the Air Force service-wide, and am particularly interested to hear how it's affecting Nellis and Creech Air Force Bases. Can you please explain how these shortfalls affect the Air Force's ability to conduct Red Flag, their main combat training exercise, and their ability to maintain UAS crews at Creech and the missions those Airmen fly overseas?

General GROSSO. Remotely Piloted Aircraft (RPA) crew manning and the impact of pilot shortfalls on Nellis AFB operations are two very distinct and separate challenges. First, with Congressional assistance, the USAF implemented a "Get Well Plan" and Continuous Process Improvement Plan (CPIP) to improve RPA crew manning and stabilize RPA operations tempo. As a result, RPA crew manning is rapidly improving and we are on glide path through FY19 to stabilize the enterprise's operations tempo. Second, the fighter pilot shortage is straining our ability to leverage the world-renowned elite training and operational capacity at Nellis AFB. Although we will not compromise the high quality tactical training Red Flag provides the USAF, joint and coalition participants, continued fighter pilot shortages may impact the way we conduct these exercises in the future. However, all exercises and sorties are currently being flown as scheduled.

Ms. ROSEN. What parts of the personnel system (for example, assignments or promotions) do you assess must be changed to aid in retention?

General GROSSO. The assignment process is one of the areas within the personnel system we are working to improve. Our pilots are leaving because they are frustrated with the lack of predictability offered under our current process. The Air Force is taking steps to increase the transparency and flexibility of the assignment process to promote family stability. Our Airmen deserve an updated assignment system that can meet manning requirements as well as ensure mission success. Therefore, a beta test is currently underway that could change how we execute assignments. This test involves the use of algorithms to optimize assignments based on the needs of the Air Force and desires of our members and their families—an assignment system for the 21st century. We are also examining alternate career paths for pilots (and other officer career fields) other than the current one-track model. The intent is to investigate the ability to offer more flexibility in how we manage and develop the force, reviewing multiple career progression options such as a technical, non-command track for pilots to allow them to concentrate on flying duties. The Air Force has also reduced additional duties, removed superfluous training courses, and hired contractors in flying squadrons to perform burdensome administrative tasks. All of these efforts allow our pilots to refocus on their primary duty: flying.

Ms. ROSEN. Will the end-strength increases in the FY 17 NDAA help with the shortage, or are there other physical barriers to increasing pilot production such as school-house size or instructor cadre?

General GROSSO. Increases in Air Force end-strength will help mitigate the pilot shortage. Two primary factors are required to produce and sustain pilots: maintainers and aircraft. The Air Force is currently more than 3,400 maintainers short. End-strength increases are critical to reducing this shortfall. A healthy maintenance force provides the foundation for operation aircraft which increases sortie production essential for making and seasoning pilots. Additional physical barriers do exist in both school-house size and instructor cadre. Air Education and Training Command (AETC) is currently growing school-house capacity from 1,200 pilots per year to approximately 1,400 pilots per year in 2020. This will be the maximum limit of pilots that can be produced at the current training bases. Air Force pilot production beyond 1,400 will require additional pilot training base to provide the necessary runways and training ranges. Looking further into the future, the Air Force must develop additional training capacity in order to increase production to 1,600 pilots annually, the amount we will need to sustain 60 fighter squadrons and mitigate pending shortfalls in other platforms. As a point of comparison, Major U.S. Airlines hired more than 4,100 pilots in 2016. Lastly, the Air Force needs to ensure a robust instructor pilot cadre to train new pilots. We look forward to working with Congress to develop retention packages that ensures the availability of these critical personnel.

Ms. ROSEN. Since flight hours are a motivator for retention, is your aircraft force structure robust and healthy enough to support all of your minimum required pilot flying hours? Will you be able to increase flying time with an increased budget or will it require more airplanes?

General GROSSO. The current pilot flying hours do not support all of the minimum training requirements. The Air Force is executing flying hour programs to the maximum efforts based on current maintenance manning and aircraft force structure. Growing Air Force end-strength which includes assessing additional aircraft maintenance capacity is critical to re-establishing a healthy maintenance foundation and making improvements to flying hour programs. In the fighter community, the current active duty force structure is too small to experience and season the required number of pilots. The Air Force requires additional fighter force structure in order to maintain a healthy fighter pilot inventory with the appropriate experience ratios. As overall pilot production numbers increase, the execution of additional flying hours within the existing training structure quickly become constrained by the limited number of existing training bases. A new basing option may be required in the 2020 timeframe to gain additional increases in production. Lastly, accelerating the acquisition of the next-generation trainer aircraft (T–X) is critical to providing additional pilot production capacity.